To Linda

Your resilience and determination on your health journey helps me moving.

I hope my story inspires you to reflect on your own pathway to success.

Warmly,

Provocative Thoughts for Daily Living

Provocative Thoughts for Daily Living

By Francisco M. Torres, MD

Provocative Thoughts for Daily Living

ISBN-13: 978-1723072109

Provocative Thoughts for Daily Living
Volume 1, First Printing September 2018
Version 1:1 (paperback edition, 5.5" x 8.5")

Publisher:

Body Works ⨍
Publications

Author: Francisco M. Torres, MD

Editor: Abby Campbell, ND/MH

Cover Designer: Ryan Munir

Contributor: Bahaa Tawik

Dedication

This book is gratefully dedicated...

to Mom, for all your hard work and sacrifices you made to make sure I had everything I needed to be successful.

to Dad, for all you did for my family and me.

"Faith and reason are like two wings on which the human spirit rises to the contemplation of truth; and God has placed in the human heart a desire to know the truth – in a word, to know himself."

Pope, John Paul II

Foreword

My Brother's Spiritual Progression

A spiritual journey is a strong metaphor for the very intimate and individual quest that someone undertakes to gain insight about life, to find out who he is, and to discover his place in existence. It is very much a process of education and discovery that happens through enlightenment. This is not a journey to find answers necessarily but more so to gain understanding. What prompts it may take many different triggers and starting points. Further, the impact and outcomes do not depend on when in life the journey begins but that it does start.

Dr. Francisco M. Torres is my younger brother, and I understand firsthand the transformation he has experienced throughout his life. In this book, he documents his own spiritual journey in an unexpected way. He uses a series of vignettes that may at first appear disconnected but end up completing a canvas of his own voyage of self-discovery, personal growth, and life insights. He shares experiences he has accumulated along his years as a healer and mentor through these snapshots of wisdom. He candidly opens his milestones of self-awareness and exposes where his journey has taken sidesteps. Every story carries a part of a puzzle that he has painstakingly pieced together along the way of his spiritual journey.

Importantly, the stories include an underlying understanding that there are certain life attributes that are outside of our control, and it is in the response to these *inevitable* that lies the path to spiritual awareness. And, there are many such unalterable certainties in life. For example: justice is not always assured... friends may sometimes let you down... we all experience aging... and then there is the problem of pain. This last example is well known to my brother as a medical professional in the management of pain.

In the vignettes dealing with this particular life challenge, he does not try to explain the existence of pain. Nor, does he develop reasons for the existence of pain or even argue that good can come of it. At its core, he rather offers a perspective that, since pain is in fact a reality of existence, the key question is more importantly how we respond to it. Rather than elaborate eschatological arguments, multiple response possibilities are presented. The related stories were born out of a lifetime of introspection from someone dedicated to the endeavor of fighting bodily pain as a medical doctor. He has found that people's response to pain reveal much about the human spirit and a pathway to greater fulfillment in life. Pain should be prevented and eliminated when possible, but it is our response in how we face it that is defining – particularly when pain, in some cases, is a path to a proportionally greater benefit.

When my brother and I were children, he and I would find ourselves in the typical sibling spats. One Saturday morning, when I was seven and he was six years old, we had a particularly strong argument (over what I can't remember). I had walked away from him and when I was some distance away, he picked up a rock and threw it at me. He did not have the intention to cause me great harm but, as it was, I turned around to look at him and the rock hit me just above the eye creating an impressive cut that quickly bathed me in blood. My father happened to be at the house and rushed me to the emergency room. He was a medical doctor and provided first aid before taking me to the hospital.

My father was the type of man that was never open about his feelings or expressive about his love. That day, he stayed with me as the hospital staff cleaned and stitched my wound. The thing that stuck with me was not the pain or fear I felt from that traumatic event. The most powerful memory was seeing the genuine concern and care in my father's face, hearing the reassuring tone of his voice, and feeling his hand holding mine. His communication was a rare instance of how I felt valued, and as such, this painful experience became a powerful anchor in our relationship. Throughout my adult life, regardless of how we interacted and his difficulty in expressing his feelings, I knew the deepness of his appreciation as well as the love of our father-son relationship. Ironically, then, a significantly painful experience became engraved in my memory as a sweet and motivating one.

The Ancient Greek philosopher, Heraclitus, maintained that the world is characterized by contrasting states. If we never fell ill, we couldn't understand what it would be to be healthy. If we never experienced hunger, we wouldn't experience the joy of eating. If wars did not happen, we couldn't appreciate the blessing of peace. If there never was a winter, we would never be able to understand when spring is arriving. Yet, it is very difficult to keep this in mind when we are traversing difficult situations, experiencing a loss, or suffering some want – whether physical or spiritual. The stories and experiences that my brother offers represent a broad and varied tapestry of situations, each presenting a perspective on a possible response, a potential attitude to take, or a perspective to embrace. They represent a firm stance that, in a world full of questions and short on answers, our thoughts and attitudes can make all the difference on what the experiences mean to us and, ultimately, how they will shape us.

In mapping his spiritual journey, my brother also defines his initial approach to the divine and his transition from a strictly religious perspective to a more freeing understanding of his own spirituality. The difference goes much further than that of the contrast between attending a specific organization with a given belief system, out of a traditional sense of duty, versus a true recognition of a reality that extends beyond strict materialism. It is more complicated and nuanced.

It is true however that often the contrast between these two possibilities leads to substantive questions and hence the dichotomy between religiosity and spirituality. In understanding the difference, it is helpful to distinguish churches from communities of faith. I like the moniker *communities of faith* because the term focuses on the value proposition from people of a same conviction, regardless of theological underpinning, coming together to support each other in their belief, being there for each other in need, and striving together to gain a deeper understanding of their theology. Unfortunately, across human history, many organized groups of faith devolved their message and theology into aberrated versions with a conscious or unrecognized aim to control and manipulate, often based on fear, leading to the negative connotation that the word *religion* carries today.

This is, of course, not an indictment on all religion, but it does accentuate the importance of having an individual journey after truth and self-discovery. Religious practices void of discovered meaning leave you exhausted and feeling inadequate. However, genuine spirituality leads to energy, purpose, and fully living in the present. This book effectively brings home the point that both bad and good experiences can be part of this learning and discovery process. If we approach everything from a perspective of learning, then that becomes the essence of mindfulness regardless of what your background has been.

These stories stand out from what would be normally expected of a *positive-thinking* or *empowerment* book based on the wide spectrum of experiences that touch on mind, body, and spirit. What you will read is more akin to a diary of my brother's spiritual progression, self-discovery, and passion for the holistic welfare of people. I invite you to participate in his adventure and gain inspiration for your own spiritual journey, whether you are deciding to start it or have been on it for years.

Dr. Juan L. Torres, PhD Biochemistry
Senior Vice President, Global Quality
Biogen Pharmaceutical

Table of Contents

Preface

Opening Myself Up

I am not a learned philosopher. I am not a yogi, a psychologist, or a motivational speaker. I am not a professional writer. I am not famous. Why me then? Because I am open to sharing and to disrupting, and because we can all learn by stopping to think about the world from time to time.

This book is a series of thoughts. They are provocative in that they are living, breathing, and changing every time you read them. These pages are a series of questions, vignettes, ideas, frustrations, and observations meant primarily to inspire both action and reflection. This book is a collection of social media posts, journal entries, emails, and mantras curated over the past several years. The stories span my life, but the writing reflects my own recent personal transformation.

I used to write books about losing weight, staying healthy, and living abundantly. With each one of them, I used my biography as motivation. The pitch went something like this:

"Fifty-seven years ago, I was born in Seville, Spain, under the dictatorship of Generalissimo, Francisco Franco. The first clear memory I have is of watching, as a child with my family, on a large black and white TV, President John F. Kennedy's funeral. I am not sure I understood the reason for the uproar then, but I was well aware of the gloominess permeating the faces in the room. I felt terrified and sad myself over the death of this man whom I didn't know, a man who had lived and died an ocean away."

From that point forward, I grew up scared, carrying the same sense of trepidation with me wherever I went. My parents raised my siblings and me with strictness, adhering to even the most archaic tenants of our Spanish-Catholic faith. I was afraid of dying and uncomfortable at any hint of change or uncertainty. I was petrified of hell.

I was also overweight. I was too shy to take my shirt off at the beach which made things difficult for me when we moved to Puerto Rico where sunbathing was a regular pastime. Growing up, I was negative about my prospects and my future. I made it through medical school only because it was expected of me, and because once I started, I had to continue until I graduated. During this time, I never stood out. I tried to hide myself from the world and the world from myself.

Just as my parents and many of my relatives had, I struggled with debilitating anxiety. Still, I always felt a special sense of untapped purpose lingering beneath the surface of fears.

It took a mild but scary cardiac event to get me going. It was as if I was being shocked back into the waking world by God or whatever forces of the universe exist. I made a dramatic physical transformation; I lost weight and toned up. But more importantly, I made a remarkable spiritual and emotional transformation.

I began to put myself out there, unashamed, for the world to see. I entered bodybuilding competitions, began to dress more brightly, and most importantly, started sharing my story.

I shared my story because I believed it could inspire others to achieve health, wellness and self-satisfaction. I quickly realized, however, that the life of the body is only part of the equation.

Marcus Aurelius collected his meditations throughout his life. They have been published and reprinted over and over and over again, century after century, because they emphasize the importance of the role of the mind in attaining peace and fulfillment. What I hope to share with you following are my own meditations, reflective of my life's experiences.

Many of the letters you're going to read in this book were written as a reminder to myself that we can change instantly when we choose to live in the present moment and when we reprogram our minds with new and uplifting beliefs. You're totally transformed when you let faith and God steer your life in the right direction.

Francisco M. Torres, MD

Part 1 –
From Physical to Spiritual

Becoming a Spiritual Athlete

Years ago now, I made an amazing physical transformation. I started choosing healthier foods. I began a new exercise regimen. I avoided habits detrimental to my cause. Over time, I became more confident of my body. I was healthier, and I felt good. I ran an ultra-marathon up Machu Picchu. I went scuba diving off the coast of Tonga. I won bodybuilding competitions and ran a successful health and wellness program for others. I was physically in the best shape of my life. Still, I was not satisfied.

My transformation had focused entirely on my body fat, muscle strength and size, and cardiovascular fitness. I had become a great athlete, but my transformation was incomplete somehow. I had forgotten to include a reworking of my spiritual body.

Everything worth achieving in this life involves incremental progress. My personal transformation was no different. Breaking bad habits takes time. Jaw-dropping results don't reveal themselves

3

overnight. On one hand, I had overcome bad habits related to night-time snacks, sugar, and physical activity. On the other hand, I needed to overcome some bad habits related to my spiritual life. So, I embarked on a path toward becoming not just a physical athlete but a spiritual one as well.

To become a spiritual athlete, I had to apply the same principles used as a physical athlete. The first step was to break bad habits – selfishness, materialism, and a constant desire to control everything. I had to *workout* spiritually as well by reading spiritual and religious texts and listening to experts on the topic. I practiced by praying daily and performing random acts of kindness frequently. I meditated on God's Word and gave up many of the complexes which had crippled me for years.

In Corinthians 3:16-17, the Lord calls our bodies the *temples of God*. We are told not to take in things that could harm what is so important to Him. We are instructed to honor and respect our bodies. The way we treat our bodies affects our spiritual health.

A fundamental insight for me has been, as the world-renowned trainer Samir Becic has explained,

> *"Spiritual awareness is one of the key components of a healthy lifestyle that impacts the whole body and rejuvenates the spirit."*

My transformation was only truly satisfying when I incorporated both types of athleticism into my life – the physical and the spiritual. In becoming a

spiritual athlete, I fulfilled the promise of all my
hard work.

Being Born Under a Dictator

It's so easy to look at a thing hundreds of times without really seeing it. My birth certificate has been hanging on the wall in my home office for nearly a decade. When I originally decorated my space, I thought it looked cool to have it hang there in the open, so ornate and colorful. A few days ago though, a little detail struck me in a brand new way.

The black eagle melted over the Spanish shield is a fascist symbol. It's a subtle reminder that I was born under General Francisco Franco's dictatorship, not so long ago, in Spain. I was too young, of course, to remember any of that time period, but noticing the eagle got me thinking. What was it like for my parents?

Did they wake up one day in a dictatorship society? Did they see it coming? Did they stock up on essentials like we do in Florida before the arrival of a hurricane? They still went out for drinks with friends, took their usual *siesta* every afternoon, went grocery shopping – didn't they? What was it like? Did they think twice about having their children born there?

Franco's dictatorship lasted a long time in Spain. It became the status quo. The secret police rounded up dissenters, homosexuals, and the disabled. Schools taught history lessons extolling fascist virtues and downplaying the Second World War. Minorities were oppressed, and the economy floundered. We weren't free, but life went on.

Rediscovering this historic stamp on my birth certificate is especially poignant for me today as my adopted country teeters on the precipice of its own new political season.

When do leaders get too strong? How easy is it to fool a population into falling in line? When is rhetoric so divisive that it becomes violent? What keeps democracies democratic?

Welcoming Uncertainty

I grew up afraid. When I was a child, I lost sleep, panicked by the prospect of changing schools or losing our home. My house was one of those where the sound of television perpetually filled in the silence of our lives. The voices of news anchors and politicians arguing over the military draft were like echoes that hunted my every day. At 10 years old, I was petrified by the thought that one day I might be drafted to fight in Vietnam.

As I became an adult, I unconsciously designed my life around security. I chose a stable career, and I also coveted a steady income, disability insurance, and a comfortable home. I avoided uncertainty and risk.

At some point, however, I realized that a life of security and comfort can actually become a gilded cage. Safety can prevent one from optimizing fulfillment and, ultimately, happiness. While I was fearful of many externalities, I let fear itself terrorize me.

In our age, we are bombarded daily by images and stories of fear. If we're constantly seeking shelter, we're constantly avoiding life. Fear is paralyzing. Instead of clinging to the shore, we should embrace adventure and dive deep into the ocean of possibility.

Sometimes, the Universe has to give us a little push to remind us of the power that jumping forward can have to change our lives for the better.

Fear is the enemy. The 32nd President of the United States, Franklin Delano Roosevelt, Sr., had it right – being uncomfortable can be rewarding. Challenges are the vehicle for growth.

Uncertainty and discomfort should never frighten us off from achieving our goals and growing as a person. Danger, risk, and faith are part of the human experience. In some ways, they are some of the most rewarding parts.

We need to break the habit and desire to cling to the past or to worry about the future. May we never let fear keep us from living. May we live in the present moment and jump.

Reaching for Excellence

I understand the value of good coaching. In fact, I swear by it. Coaches train us to grow into better versions of ourselves whether it be in the sports, music, or business world. They guide us into territory that we've never sought and teach us how to succeed.

Early in my life, I knew I wanted to become a doctor. I spent a summer in high school interning at a local hospital, shadowed physicians in the emergency room while asking for advice and taking notes so that I could be a great physician myself one day. I regarded the direction of these great physicians and put them to good use. Now, I have practiced medicine for over 30 years.

Throughout my career, I continued to learn from and incorporate the skills of other doctors – even through my own innovation and expansion with new forms of patient care. However, my career was only one piece of my life's puzzle.

11

Since I was young, I struggled to stay healthy. My parents were overweight and, unfortunately, nobody in my family was a good model of wellness. Outside of my profession, this deficiency translated to other areas of my life. I lacked confidence, energy, and drive. So, I sought out motivation to help drive me to excellence.

This is when I discovered famous life coaches, such as Tony Robbins and Robin Sharma. I followed them until I felt capable of achieving my own personal wellness goals.

A few years back, I decided to run the vaunted Machu Picchu Ultra-Marathon which took me through the Inca ruins in Peru – nearly 14,000 feet at the highest elevation. This was going to be a great feat, so I turned to others for help. Just as I sought help when I wanted to be a doctor, I consulted experts in high-altitude training and extreme marathons so that they could help shape my plan as I wanted to succeed with excellence.

Another time a few years ago, I decided to enter a stage competition for physique bodybuilding. I was 52-years old, and this was going to be my first competition. For this, I relied heavily on coaches and trainers who had forged the path already. I learned from them, and I was able to translate that training with a little hard work into a victory.

I strongly believe that we all need somebody to guide us, reminding and motivating us in our goals to excellence. Even the most successful professionals and talented people can benefit from targeted and personalized guidance.

The successes I've had in life were sprung from some of the best coaches and, today, I continue to benefit from coaching in my own life.

Sparking Curiosity

Recently, I drove to the music store to buy a new violin bow. My current bow cost 75 dollars, and the next model was 200 dollars. Later, I started wondering if a more expensive bow might bring a smoother sound.

I'm no virtuoso – at least not yet – so I turned to the music experts for advice. Watching a YouTube video featuring one of the world's preeminent violinists, she posed this question:

> *"Can you tell the difference when I play a $500 violin bow versus the times I play with a $160,000 one?"*

No, that wasn't a typo. She actually said "$160,000." Though she was shocking about the price tag, she never gave an answer to the question. Instead, she leaves the viewer to decide.

So, I started thinking about this. After all, there aren't any monuments erected to famous paint brushes, right? Is it an oversight or an insight? We reserve praise for the workman, not the tools... the painter, not the paintbrush... the violinist, not her violin bow. By listening to the famous violinist, would you know that her violin bow is much more expensive than mine? Whether it's 500 or 160,000 dollars? You would say she's a marvelous violinist, and you'd know that I am not – at least not yet!

I sort of identify with the anonymity of instruments. As human beings, we are instruments of God. We are tools of kindness, excellence, compassion, and brotherhood. We often do good anonymously, and we don't ask to be praised for the masterpieces we help bring about. After all, that praise belongs to God. In some ways, I think that makes us heroic:

> *"We aren't good because it's popular or because we are lauded. We are good according to our own value, whether anybody knows it or not."*

Finding Faith through Suffering

The first night home after running an ultra-marathon in Peru, I drove to the hospital to visit a good friend who was suddenly ill. On the car ride over, all I could think about was how fleeting her health was. It was surreal that I was just climbing a mountain at high altitude the day before when all along my friend, Sandy, was laying here in the hospital bed relying on a machine to breathe and keep her alive. She was much younger than me, and she was clinging to a life she had once lived vibrantly. Sandy was a lovely person who brought joy to my life.

Once I entered the hospital room and saw my friend, the sad thoughts escaped me. Sandy and I joked like old time and reminisced about the baseball games (Phillies and Rays) we enjoyed together. We talked about old times at work. We even talked about *death* which seemed to have found a home with her family. Her husband, Angelo, had died not long before. However, she had

17

other deaths in the family as well. Sandy didn't complain though. She just wondered *why?*

The family tragedies that Sandy had over the few months before she got sick made me think of Job in the Bible who was a just, kind, loving man. However, he was plagued by physical suffering, torture, and death for absolutely no apparent reason. He got horrible sores on his body, and his farms were destroyed by vermin. Worst of all, he lost 10 of his children. Everyone around tells him said that he was justified to be angry and curse God for all the pain inflicted upon him.

Being the patient and humble man that he was, Job refused that temptation. Instead, he begged God for understanding. He didn't curse or hate. He just wondered.

God then sent his voice from the skies and told Job that man cannot ever understand the ways of God, and that faith and trust are what sustain him through the bad times. If we were only so lucky that the clouds would open up, and God would speak to us!

However, I think the story is supposed to tell us that the bad in our lives is no reflection on anything we've done. It isn't distributed evenly amongst everyone, and most of the time, it's not even done purposefully. It's just a reminder that in our suffering, we can find faith – faith that we are a part of something much larger and that the suffering will one day blossom into forgiveness and understanding.

Sandy loved her husband, and she loved her father whom she also lost. She carried the pain of their loss with her daily until the day she died. However, Sandy left this world as no stranger to death. Just as death took away what she cared about most, it's also given her back what it took away. I would like to think Sandy is no longer suffering and happily reunited with her loved ones somewhere. Still yet, I now wonder.

I don't think there is a logical answer to the human mind of why we suffer. People much smarter and saintly than me have tried and failed to explain it, but I think that's maybe the beauty in pain. Some things are beyond our understanding, and perhaps they serve as windows into the greater universe around us.

Suffering is possibly the greatest testimony of love, an artifact of a life lived in joy.

Relating Better

One day, a woman called my office to say she would prefer to be seen by another physician. Though I was surprised, I'd be lying if I said this was the first time one of my patients has questioned my medical advice. However, this particular phone call was unusual for another reason.

The woman wanted me to recommend another physician who was less *fit* than me. I was taken aback by her request, but her rationale was that she didn't think I could be sympathetic to her condition. She described herself as a 55-year old woman with a *broken body*, and she felt that I couldn't possibly relate to her.

I have to admit that at first this seemed absurd. I've recommended specialists before, but I've never referred a patient to another doctor based on his or her appearance.

I've always thought that having a healthy doctor motivated patients. Never did I imagine that some would be intimidated. Does a physician's healthy lifestyle even affect his patients in a positive manner anymore?

I always thought that an overweight doctor was a hypocrite if he recommended diet and exercise. After all, why would a patient want to follow a doctor's advice if the doctor can't follow his own advice? Is this the type of doctor that can truly sympathize with his patient?

I would think an athletic doctor who recommends diet and exercise is a great example. After all, fit physicians understand the benefits of a healthy lifestyle. Plus, they have the knowledge of how to obtain it. Then again, I'm not the patient who called me but this did cast a dilemma.

Personally, I want to motivate my patients to be well. It's important for me to wean my patients from their old excuses and challenge them to take charge of their health. At the same time, I want to be relatable to my patients as well.

Changing for the Better

I've been on a journey of self-discovery, pushing myself further than ever to be fully accountable for my own actions and results. Through this process over the years, I've learned a lot about myself and continue to learn more almost every day.

With the challenges and awareness this journey has brought me, it has also created some unexpected circumstances that have challenged me to grow.

In both my personal and professional lives, I have become more aware of my daily interactions and how they impact my life. Some people, even very close family and friends, have shown me their challenges – mostly subconsciously. Unfortunately, this clashes with me personally as I become stronger and more aware.

I've also inadvertently attracted people to me who are completely unaware of themselves. In their ineptness, I became their lifeline because I had already figured out how to succeed.

Awkwardly, this leaves me in a situation where I need to learn how to coach my immediate family and circle of friends. I need to help them become more aware of themselves and their surroundings.

Unfortunately, this is far from my area of expertise or knowledge. If I don't help though, I'm afraid and certain that I will grow more distant from these people as I continue to move forward.

I am changing, hopefully for the better. My hope is that the people around me will too.

Taking My Own Advice

One afternoon in 2008, I rushed myself to the local emergency room as I had experienced serious chest pain. With certainty, I thought I was suffering a heart attack. The initial diagnosis was tentative but affirmed my suspicions. This made me panic. However, further testing showed that I didn't actually have a heart attack. Rather, I was having non-specific changes in my cardiovascular system. At that time, I was 30 pounds overweight and was not involved in any type of exercise routine. My heart just wasn't being conditioned the way it should have been, and I needed to make changes to become healthy.

However, the impetus to change my life goes back much further than the day I thought I was having a heart attack. As a child, I was chronically overweight and suffered throughout my school years from bullying. I had a low self-esteem. Eating became a source of comfort, an easy way to temporarily calm my anxieties. This was a vicious habit that unfortunately continued into my adulthood.

As an adult, I lost significant weight at times. However, my weight fluctuated. I would get in great shape, and I'd be right back where I started six months later.

After my heart event, it was time to get in shape once and for all. Not only did my physical transformation help my heart and give me energy. I was able to participate fully in life from my relationships to business. Best of all, I became much happier.

As a doctor, I have come to realize that I cannot help my patients if I don't take care of myself first. So often, caretakers give priority to other people in their lives – all the while forgetting about caring for themselves. Because I work with several patients each day, I see this often. However, many of these people have much more serious problems with their health than I ever did. They are bombarded with chronic disease that is difficult to turn back. Forgetting to care for self is a huge mistake (especially for a physician).

Though I wasn't the greatest health example in my earlier years of being a doctor, I know that I couldn't be the exceptional doctor I am today if it weren't for my heart event. I now take care of my own wellbeing – both physically and emotionally. By having more energy and mental awareness, I can attend to the needs of my patients better. Best of all, I can show them that change is really possible.

If you're one who has difficulty changing, just remember this:

*"If there should be a change in cabin
pressure, put on your own oxygen mask
first before helping others."*

If you don't take care of yourself first, you may not
know how to by the time you've helped everyone
else. Don't wait for extreme emergencies to start
making yourself priority. By living your life on your
own terms – by respecting and treating your body
with care and love – you save your dignity.

Seeking My Intuition

Albert Einstein, the German-born physicist who developed the special and general theories of relativity and won the Nobel Prize for Physics in 1921, once said:

> *"I believe in intuitions and inspirations... I sometimes feel that I am right. I do not know that I am."*

As logical people, can we recognize the power of intuition as being real? Is intuition something that we all possess but are afraid to utilize for our own good and for the benefits of others?

I believe that intuition is a part of our spirit that we may have forgotten how to use. Our society is predominantly left-brain dominated, often avoiding things that can't be explained scientifically through the senses.

We all have the ability to be intuitive by reconnecting with our inner selves and awakening those powers. It takes practice, but diving deeper into our thoughts provides us the ability to develop our intuition and helps us become more comfortable when faced with challenging decisions.

However, we must not confuse being intuitive with being afraid. We may have a feeling of uneasiness when we're ready to embark on a new venture, but this is just a feeling of anxiety when facing the unknown or uncertainty.

The only way to know the difference between fear and intuition is to look deep inside of ourselves and see how each emotion makes us feel.

> *"When we think about the situation we find ourselves in, should we expand or contract? Do we let fear set in, or do we seize the opportunity to let our intuition lead the way?"*

That is one of the reasons I use activity-related meditation to get in touch with my body and pay attention to its reaction.

> *"Prayer is telephoning to God, and intuition is God telephoning to us."*

After practicing medicine for more than 30 years, I have to admit that a large percentage of my clinical decisions are based on intuition and not just thousands of past experiences and subconscious knowledge of the situation.

Recently in my life, I have been guided to utilize my intuition instead of my logic to make powerful decisions. Being guided by intuition, the world becomes a big playground in which I am constantly on recess. By trusting intuition, life becomes more beautiful and experiences are enhanced. We must trust our intuition.

Using Time Wisely

I used to think I didn't have time for anything outside of work and family obligations. Just a few years ago, I certainly couldn't imagine carving out time to write a book, let alone five. Somewhere between then and now, I learned something profound about my time though.

Did you know that the average person will probably spend 10 years of life watching television? Ten years is the average!

Who wants to be average? Extraordinary people don't do ordinary things. Watching television has become the typical thing that keeps most people ordinary and struggling beneath the surface to break out and be extraordinary.

People with the most *radical* ideas – Thomas Edison, Nikola Tesla, the Wright brothers, and Albert Einstein – are often ridiculed as crazy or weird. They don't do ordinary things like most.

Somehow though, they're the ones we remember. They're the ones we describe as *special*. Why? I can't say for sure, but I bet they didn't spend 20 percent of their lives watching television.

Just imagine! Instead of watching television, that time was spent learning a new language, reading, or just thinking. How many *radical* ideas could be devised doing these things?

Over time, I've made television less and less a part of my life. It no longer constrains me, nor does it feel like an obstacle to my time anymore. Because of this, I have found myself thinking and learning more. I'm even interacting more. The extra time I now have for reflection has also led to increased innovation. I feel lighter, as well as more thoughtful and in touch with the world.

We don't have to give up television or watching movies altogether, but being mindful of the minutes we dedicate to something can be a blessing. Spending time on things that are more fruitful in life can help us accomplish great things, build relationships, and start something extraordinary.

Coaching as Leader

Everyone has advice on how we should improve our relationships, lose weight, earn more money, or improve memory. Even television infomercials are saturated with lectures on how to do things better.

Every *Joe Schmo* with a Wi-Fi connection has something to say on social media about how we're living our lives. I've even found numerous bookstores stuffed with shelves of *how to* books and manifestos proclaiming the *12 keys to success* – including my own, *12 Practical Steps to a New You Forever*. What gives?

> *"But, Dr. T! Isn't that basically what you do with your newsletters and your books? Is there is a catch?"*

Very shrewd, Grasshopper! Please let me offer a distinction.

> *"If you aren't coaching, you aren't leading. The problem is that most of us don't know what real coaching looks like."*

Coaching isn't just telling people what to do. We've all had those coaches, whether it be on the football field or at work – those who bark out orders and don't take their own advice. They project their opinions onto others and ultimately do little more than disempower the members of their team. They want to replace your thinking with theirs.

We think of coaches in the same way we might think of managers – at the top of the organization. However, leadership doesn't come from position.

Managers develop visions and task others on how to make those visions become reality. They measure others in terms of their ability to accomplish success in the framework the manager establishes.

Coaching is not managing. It is not about setting rigid expectations or restricting subordinates to follow their lead. Like the famous American basketball coach of a Catholic high school, Morgan Wooten, once said about coaching:

> *"It's about treating your team as you would treat your family."*

Coaching opens up success to its followers. It's about sharing experiences, collaborating goals, and being flexible. Coaching is about inspiration, not direction.

As a coach myself, I hope to be an inspiration to my clients and followers as they develop their own goals and build their own success. In turn, my goal is to grow with them which will make me even better at coaching.

Growing My Life

A few years back, I spent some time in Toronto, Canada, with one of my favorite idols and mentors, Robin Sharma. He is one of the world's leading motivational speakers and leadership coaches. You may recognize him as an author as he's countless books on achievement and success, including the bestselling *The Monk Who Sold His Ferrari* and *The Leader Who Had No Title*.

It was an exciting adventure to be with this great man, and I was honored to talk with him one-on-one during an evening of dinner. In fact, this was a life changing experience for me. I returned home with a completely different outlook about life and purpose.

Following are some of the things that Robin shared that helped me that may help you.

1. You must train your brain to be more creative and eliminate distraction.

2. What gets scheduled gets done.

3. Clarity is the mother of mastery.

4. When you write your goals down on a piece of paper, you activate the motor part of your cerebral cortex to execute what is important to you.

5. The number one defining factor in success is GRIT. Keep the faith in your dream, and believe in yourself when no one else does.

6. Focus your time to make things happen and to be of service to others. Want your kids to remember you as a dreamer, as someone who was devoted and encouraging.

Between 5 to 6 o'clock in the morning, or when you wake up, write in you journal every morning. It's the *Holy Hour*. Write about where you're at, what you want this year to look like, what's more important in your life and your values, what you're feeling and thinking, and where you want to go.

Sharing My Thoughts on Social Media

Just by reading my book, you've probably gathered that I love to share. While some people enjoy that about me, others find it suspicious. Then there are many who just don't really think all that much about it.

I am not a millennial like my children. Unlike them, I didn't come out of the womb texting or browsing Facebook or Twitter. Over the past several years, however, I have discovered the full force of the internet.

I don't share my thoughts because I think they're so important. I'm not quite that narcissistic, nor do I share my thoughts because I think they'll change the minds of people who think differently than me. I'm not quite that optimistic. Instead, I share my thoughts to remind people who already think the way I do. That's the beauty of sharing, especially on a platform as far-reaching and wide-ranging as social media.

39

Sometimes, it's nice to remember that others share the same feelings, wonders, and sadness. Though there are many negative aspects to the internet's rapid proliferation, I still believe it's a net positive if it puts any dent at all into the ubiquitous challenge of human loneliness.

Sure, sharing can be a sign of self-importance. However, it can also be a sign of generosity and vulnerability. We don't have to believe we're the smartest, most interesting or insightful person on the planet for our words to mean something.

Then there are some of us who face doubts and fears about our own significance. Yet, we shouldn't let this stop us from doing what we love – especially if what we love has the potential to improve someone else's life.

Social media is not for everyone, but at least for now, it is for me.

Handling Strife

Have you ever gotten this advice?

> *"Remove the negative influences from your life."*

I've gotten that same advice many times, and the theory is sound. Practicing this kind of removal, however, is much more difficult to wrap my head around.

Recent times have been one of discovery for me, and I've learned a lot about myself. I've defined goals, confronted fears, tackled biases, and forged a new path. It's been a time of self-realization. However, it has had an outward impact as well. Not everyone is on the same trajectory, and it shows.

So when one of my mentors tells me to quite simply remove the negative influences from my life, I find myself in an increasingly troubling predicament.

Negative influences can be many different things. Trashy television being one, and fast food might be another. However, the most pervasive negative influence for any of us, and certainly for me, is the people whose negativity surround us.

Sometimes those people are acquaintances. Other times, they are co-workers. They may even be old friends or family. With this context, the advice to removing negative influences can become almost cruel and heartbreaking.

As I continue to grow into the kind of person I can be proud of, the contrast with my negative friends and family becomes more pronounced. Interactions are now strained – presumably because in my transformation, they recognize their own challenges more acutely (mostly subconsciously, I believe).

I don't think this is jealousy or resentment towards me as much as it is the fear of failure in themselves. I believe this can sometimes manifest itself in cynicism and, ultimately, negativity. Unfortunately, that negativity is a growing impact on my own life.

Fortunately, I can adjust with some people. The relationship changes, and modifications can be make for interactions to suit my new awareness levels. However, it can be far more challenging with others.

What do I do when the people I love cause me strife? Grievously, it isn't as simple as cutting out the negative.

Do I become a coach? How does that approach change my ties with friends and family? Is it my place to intervene? Do I fashion myself a role model and fight the influence? Do I ignore the person altogether?

I don't know the solution to this dilemma. Looking into my future, I worry that I'll become more distant from these people as I change. Maybe that's the price of progress.

Yet, I don't want to believe that just yet. Even those who are cynical about my transformation have value to add in my life. If nothing else, the bonds I share with friends and family are too strong to simply remove.

I do believe I am changing for the better and that the impulse to remove negativity from my life is a powerful one. This goes for you as well.

However, the question remains:

> *"How can we remove negativity effectively with those people who are close to us? How can we keep our relationships strong, even as we recognize the drawbacks in doing so?"*

Caring for Gaudete

Not long ago, I was in search of a puppy to bring into my home. I daydreamed about this new member of my family, and I put some concerted effort into coming up with a name for him or her. If you've ever raised a pet or had a child, you know that choosing a name can be quite the existential challenge. After all, a name says a lot.

For example, take the name *Fido*. It's a classic, almost cartoonish, common moniker for man's best friend. Fido itself originates from the Latin word *fifes* which means trustworthiness or protection. It's at the root of words like fidelity and confidante, and it's the perfect fit for the loyal family pet.

Recently, I received a copy of the Vatican's latest Apostolic Exhortation, written by Pope Francis. It's called *Gaudete et exsultate*. The word, Gaudete, captured my imagination as I had heard it before in old prayers and hymns at mass. I never knew what it meant, so I conducted a little research.

In Latin, Gaudete is the imperative form of a word that means to rejoice, to act, or to do something. It's a commandment to experience joy. It urges us not to wait passively for something or someone to make us joyful. It exhorts us to find and experience joy in our daily lives.

The frustrated psychiatrist in me began to wonder how I might make this word useful when others are depressed, listless, hopeless, or even desperate. Is it imperative to find joy? Does it involve engaging in acts of selflessness and love? Does it involve a conscious appreciation of good in the world?

The apostle Paul once said, "Dismiss all anxiety from your minds." Jesus preached that perfect love casts all fear, which is something deeply rooted in anxiety and depression. The opposite of love is not hate. In fact, He taught us that it is fear.

Anxiety, in many instances, comes from the conviction that we are in charge of our own lives. It comes from the belief that there's nothing or no one above us that can help alleviate our emotional or spiritual burdens. By naming my new puppy Gaudete or *Gaudi* (like the artist, for short), I will be reminded on a daily basis to be joyful and to practice an act of love when caring for him.

Learning from My Children

I think most people aim to guide their children. After all, that dynamic makes sense. As parents, we see ourselves as experienced and mature. We know best.

However, I'm starting to see this traditional dynamic a little differently. I'm opening up my relationship with my children and starting to reverse the student-teacher dynamic.

For years, I've sought guidance from some of the most renowned thinkers in the personal success industry including Anthony Robbins, Deepak Chopra, Robin Sharma, and Christian Simpson. But when I stop to think about it, nothing they have taught me can hold a torch to what I've learned from my children.

Without my kids, I wouldn't know a homerun from a touchdown. Thanks to my children, I've had very important person (VIP) tours of the best universities in the world. I've toured the professional baseball leagues of the United States

47

and Puerto Rico. I've even travelled to a number of states I would have otherwise never dreamed of visiting.

My children have allowed me to share my own experiences with them, but they still pale in comparison to the life lessons my boys have taught me. I've learned from them as they overcome modern challenges. I've suffered their pain as they've struggled and been amazed as they have inevitably overcome. I've seen them innovate and imagine new lives for themselves and even seen them reinvent friendships and impress others in ways I can't even understand. My children have been, and remain, the most profound teachers in my life.

Too often, we project our own brand of wisdom and knowledge onto our kids without absorbing everything they have to share with us in return. It's important to pass on what we know, but it's just as important to recognize what we don't know from them. The famous martial artist and actor, Bruce Lee, said it best:

> *"A good teacher protects his pupils from his own influence."*

We mustn't be afraid to influence or be afraid to let ourselves be influenced by our children. We can teach them a lot by our examples, but we can learn just as much, if not more, by theirs. Just like my children, I'm sure yours can also teach you how to deal with stress and how to thrive in the midst of new challenges.

Laughing at Mistakes

We all do stupid and embarrassing things from time to time. Even the inspirational writer, William Arthur Ward, said:

> *"To make mistakes is human; to stumble is commonplace; to be able to laugh at yourself is maturity."*

After a recent trip with my family, I was flustered about getting to the airport on time. I have four boys, so packing can be quite an operation. While going through the security checkpoint, I panicked. I began frantically patting my pant and jacket pockets.

> *"My backpack! My backpack! Where's my backpack?"*

My four boys laughed. For one thing, my backpack was where it was supposed to be – on my back. For another, my family derived inestimable pleasure from how earnestly I had searched my pockets for my very full-sized backpack.

For weeks, this was the joke du jour in my family. Whenever anything was lost, they frenetically started patting themselves down.

"Where's my computer?"

Hilariously, everyone would immediately search their pockets. Even when I asked where one of my sons was, the others would feign despair and perform the ritual dance before answering.

Eventually, I began to resent the jokes. They were obviously making fun of me and my mistake. Then my resentment turned into anger. Most people have probably experienced it – humiliation, impatience, and pride. These things conspire to prevent us from embracing and even appreciating our own fallibility.

Eventually, my children's laughter caused me to lash out at them. I was tired and just wanted to sit on the couch and watch television before going to bed. It was late, but the kids were wide awake.

When I couldn't find the television remote, the boys pounced. They all started shouting, "The remote! The remote!" and began patting themselves down – pockets, shoulders, legs, and shoes. I just lost it, and screamed at them while storming off. Not my finest hour!

Do you ever get really angry at someone or something, when in fact, who you're really annoyed at is yourself due to your own stupidity?

After I cooled down, I had to reflect. What was I so angry about? What were my sons pointing out about me that made me so upset?

The answer is simple, really. The jokes were scratching away at my fragile ego. A momentary lapse in rational judgment – a moment of panic – had turned into a full-scale assault on my own self-worth. How crazy is that?

Upon reflection, I realized that I didn't fail because I didn't realize I already had my backpack, or because I lost control with my boys due to them making fun of me. I failed because I couldn't find my ability to laugh at my own mistake. Unfortunately, this was an unhealthy attachment to an image of myself – a prideful image of myself.

Knowing this, I took an opportunity I couldn't resist. After dinner one night, we were walking out of a restaurant. As we stepped into the parking lot, I stopped walking. Everyone took a few steps before they realized I had fallen behind. When they turned around to find me, I began ostentatiously patting myself down, searching my pockets, the back of my pants, my shoulders – then exclaimed:

"Where's the car?"

That night, I laughed harder than anyone.

We should never allow our ego to get in the way of enjoying our mistakes or preventing ourselves from learning, growing, and laughing. We're all fallible as mistakes happen. To err, after all, is human.

Focusing on Great Love

Grand donations and heroic acts of selflessness stand out in the memories of the masses, and they should. It should not, however, discourage us from performing our own acts of charity each day. We must support our friends and foes alike and practice selflessness like a morning routine.

When I was younger, I dreamed of changing the world like Dr. Albert Schweitzer, the late French-German theologian, philosopher, and humanitarian. I wanted to donate money and be a renowned motivational speaker.

However, I soon realized that, as important as philanthropy is, it just wasn't in my path. I didn't want to be comfortable by throwing money at uncomfortable images on the television. Instead, I wanted to do something more.

Each act of kindness is worth more than any money I could ever give. Each kind word said to someone in my office carries more weight than the most impactful speech of the most famous motivational speaker. Each patient, friend, or acquaintance I treat with humility, respect, and benevolence add together a sum greater than any donation I could ever give. The great French philosopher said it best:

> *"A soul in affliction finds it difficult to love anything. It must therefore almost force itself to keep loving God and others or at least wanting to love, although it may only be an infinitesimal part of itself."*

Seeing the Door Wide Open

Many parents will openly discuss their dreams for their children. However, it becomes an uncomfortable topic when those dreams become more unreachable.

For me, I wanted my son to become a Major League baseball player. In a way, I wanted it for myself – not truly for him. I found out the hard way that you cannot control destiny or expect things to go according to plan.

Being robbed of the game myself at such a young age only fueled my anxiety and stress that came with my dreams for my son. Unfortunately, those dreams were followed by disappointment. I was a kid again, being let down by the game I had loved so much – for a second time.

At that time, I had no idea that I was eventually going to be prouder than I ever could have been right then.

My son, Gabe, works in the professional baseball system. By traveling to different stadiums and meeting with people from across the country, he works hard on and off the field. Though he doesn't take batting practice or field groundballs, he helps mold those that do. Training them to be faster, stronger, and tougher are just a few of his job requirements.

I think of Gabe heading to the Major League facilities, and I reflect on my dream for him. I always used to think of this as *our* dream but his life.

The dream is being fulfilled right now, and I frequently speak of him as entering the Major Leagues through the *back door*, but maybe this isn't the back door after all. It's just a different door, adjacent to the one I had in my mind's eye for over 20 years – with shiny door handles and all.

Both doors were always in front. However, the door my son walked through – the door that leads to the fresh-cut grass and newly wetted clay through the weight room – that door was left wide open.

Balancing Life

Towards the end of my medical residency, my wife and I began having children. We had three young boys by the time I finished my one-year fellowship. My wife was also a medical resident at that time. We worked hard and were lucky to have parents who pitched in from time to time to help. The daycare near our home was also a blessing. Still, we missed out on a great deal of our boys' lives.

My boys weren't quite in school yet when we moved to Florida where I began working at my first practice. As my wife and I continued to grow in our careers, we struggled to balance our professions with our family life.

We were often late picking the boys up (four in total) from sport practices, and we missed games and recitals. We came home late from time to time, so food always had to be prepared in the mornings using a slow cooker – which was usually my wife's brilliant work. Though we wanted to build our professions, we loved our family.

I've often been told that a robust family life isn't compatible with an exceptional business life. I've also heard that sacrifices are made with each gain. There's a notion that our professional and personal lives sit on two dependent scales. By removing time or attention from one to give to the other alters the balance in an objective way. In other words, being the best father is impossible when being the most successful businessman, and vice versa.

However, I believe this scale analogy completely misses the point. After all, we all have a drive and a purpose in life. No matter how acute the drive is today, the realization that one business or even one child isn't some *singular* life's work.

We are the sum of our parts. Unfortunately, we can't be all things to all people. Nor can we be everywhere at once. Concern about time and focus are legitimate, yet time and attention are always demanded. Children, spouses, parents, friends, hobbies, and addictions make up those demands.

No matter how focused we are, we can't be myopic about our lives. What's important is not how much time or attention we sacrifice in our businesses in order to have children, or vice versa. But, what's most important is happiness, and I can tell you from experience – and I'm in my 50s now – that happiness is what helps fulfill life's purpose.

As a father, I was absent from time to time. And, on the side of business, I ducked out of meetings early to catch the tail end of one of my boys' soccer or baseball games. My kids have resented me, and they have adored me. My business has flourished, and it has floundered. Throughout though, I have been fulfilled, and my drive remains. Despite my shortcomings, I'm happy that my boys are enjoying their own successes now.

My oldest son is a Harvard Law graduate and a United States Naval officer. The next two in line work in professional baseball – one as a coach and the other as a player. The youngest is attending Brown University, following his oldest brother's footsteps. I know that part of their drive is due to witnessing mine. I could have taken more time off to be with them (maybe I should have), but life's circumstances made them into the young men they are today – motivated, professionally persevering, and successful.

Professional success can enhance our children's lives. On the other hand, they will motivate us to be better bosses, entrepreneurs, and people. Being a better professional can make a better parent, and vice versa – if we allow it.

Not everyone wants to have children, and I'm not advocating this one way or another. However, life's achievements are diffuse. Success is not conditioned on one thing or another. In fact, the most successful people are the ones who embrace the chaos of their multifaceted lives and channel energy into purpose – both business and personal wise.

Anyone can be a great entrepreneur, as well as a great parent. Both are linked for those who have children. Life may not always seem perfect, but it's not a zero-sum choice. It's an opportunity to take on something new and challenging, and it could ultimately be something very rewarding. Making the choice that makes the best sense is the way to go, but we must do it with the broader purpose in mind.

Discovering Truth behind My Transformation

Each new year, I put together an annual promotional calendar with pictures of myself. This occasion begs me to pause and reflect on the incredible journey it has taken me to arrive where I am today.

Over 10 years ago, my physical transformation began. However, the fact is this moment was in the making much longer. In digging through hundreds of my *before* photos, I'm reminded of the many false starts and the myriad of unfulfilled intentions to which I subjected myself before I was finally ready to change my life forever.

In reviewing these images of my former self, I recall the desire I had to transform my body. However, I also recall the lack of true commitment that prevented me from achieving my ultimate success.

I spent years trying to complete weight loss contests, acting on my desire in bursts and then

61

failing flat again in a never-ending cycle of regret and disappointment.

It took my cardiac incident of 2008 to ignite a true fire in me. I discovered that change had to be emotional and spiritual before it could become physical and long lasting. When I sort through the images of the new me, I don't just see a new body. I see a more holistic sort of strength. I see the commitment to myself that simply did not exist in me before. I see a new person.

The *before and after* pictures are impressive. Anyone can see the great physical changes in my chest, arms, and abdomen. However, I see a new heart and a clear mind. In the end, that's the truly the most remarkable transformation.

Viewing Life like a Bird

The ancient Greek philosopher, Plato, once said:

> *"Whenever you want to talk about people, it's best to take a bird's view and see everything all at once."*

I love that! Have you ever flown on a plane and looked out the window to see the world below? I have. As the wheels retreat into the plane and the wings take me gliding over mountain ranges and city lights, I realize just how small I am. I am like a bird.

It's at that moment that I no longer feel overwhelmed by overbearing responsibilities of the modern world. I am focused only on one thing – my inner self. Suddenly, I am content with my life, and an overwhelming feeling of inner peace takes over. I realize that from a bird's view, everything appears dwarfed and inconsequential.

The cars are like toys, and the buildings are like Legos. In that moment, they are insignificant and trivial. Before flying, my problems and adversaries seemed insurmountable but shrink after take-off. I find a new perspective.

Is this how the world must look to God? Maybe that's why all the religious leaders preach forgiveness and love. They see the world from up above; they see it from a bird's eye view.

Whatever problems we encounter through life, we should take a moment to be like a bird flying high above them all. Our problems cannot touch us, nor do they matter there. No matter how big a problem might seem on the ground, imagine how small it is thousands of feet above. Everything can be solved with love and forgiveness in that place.

Visiting the Holy Land

Recently, I spent 10 days visiting the Holy Land of Israel. It was there that I realized that I grew up feeling scared, uncomfortable with change and the unknown as afraid of dying.

Growing up in a strict Spanish, Catholic family had multiple challenges. It brought about guilt and fear that dominated my mind for most of my life. I was fearful of sinning and paying the ultimate prize - HELL. I was also afraid of breaking rules being different from the norm.

My parents were great people. They were born with limited tools and beliefs, and they were looking for purpose in life as well as a sense of significance. For them, religion became their driving force.

After moving to Puerto Rico as a kid, I was confronted with other challenges. Mental disease was prevalent on my dad's side of the family, and my own mother gradually succumbed to its powerful tentacles. At the end of her life, her face was a living testimony of what years of mental anguish can do to a person. My dad was also the victim of undiagnosed mental illness.

Because of this, a negative atmosphere permeated my life for many years. I carried a constant feeling of sadness and defeat during my school years. However, I showed an attitude of happiness and security to others. Because of my sadness, I was always envisioning a different me. Though I believe it was my strong will power and positive sense of visualization that brought me through.

My trip to the Holy Land served as a reminder that I can change at any moment when I choose to live in the present moment. Will and reprogramming my mind with new and uplifting beliefs is how I can overcome the hardships of the past.

Most of all, tremendous help comes from God when we allow Him to steer our lives in the right direction. Even during my down times and lack of self-esteem, I knew that I was special to Him. He gives me, and you, that very strong sense of purpose to live joyfully. We just need to listen to that still, small voice.

Never Settling for Lukewarm

Do you ever hear *Happy New Year* with the thought of God vomiting on a pinball machine? Well, it happened to me one morning.

When I was a kid, I loved to play pinball at the videogame arcade. Quarter after quarter, I'd play in hopes to win a free game so that I could keep playing.

My dream was to become a *pinball master*. Unfortunately, I was not very good at playing. In fact, I was pretty bad at the game. When I ran out of coins after a half hour or so, I would leave the arcade longing to go back again just to try my efforts at becoming that master.

One afternoon, I didn't need any quarters to play. The coin box was malfunctioning, so I got to play for free. Unafraid of losing, I kept playing game after game. It put me in a trance as I continually played over and over again. I was like a pinball *junkie*.

As I continued to play, my fingers eventually operated separately from my brain to where I didn't even know what I was doing anymore. After a while, I lost interest in the game. It just wasn't enjoyable anymore. In fact, I got tired of playing pinball, as my penchant for it was overcome by indifference and apathy. Funny! That was all it took.

Going back to my thought of God vomiting on a pinball machine, I wondered what that meant. Could it have anything to do with being *lukewarm*?

In the Book of Revelations, God laments when his followers are lukewarm.

> *"Because you are lukewarm and neither hot nor cold, I will vomit you out of My mouth."*

As a physician, I am very familiar with inducing vomit as a treatment to purge poison. So, why does God need to vomit us out when we are lukewarm? Even more, what does it have to do with *pinball* and the *New Year*?

Being lukewarm means being half-hearted. It reflects a failure to commit, and this happens when we are hesitant in our convictions and complacent about our passions.

As much as I was addicted to pinball, I wasn't really committed to it. I was never going to be the expert I wanted to be because my passion for it was lukewarm. It only took a few free games to teach me that.

Going forward, I want to think about all the ways I have been lukewarm in the past, as well as all the ways I can be *hot or cold* in the future. No one wants a lukewarm drink, so why settle for a lukewarm life?

Striving for Greatness

I love proverbs. Being timeless, they are thought provoking. Consider this Hindu proverb for a moment:

> *"Help your brother's boat across, and your own will reach the shore."*

You've probably heard variations of this proverb, such as when the 35th United States President, John F. Kennedy, said:

> *"A rising tide lifts all boats."*

Even though he was talking about economics, it certainly applies to a lot of other situations.

American author and motivational speaker, Zig Ziglar, notes:

> *"You can have everything in life you want, if you will just help enough other people get what they want."*

Twentieth century self-help author, Napoleon Hill, once said:

> *"It is literally true that you can succeed best and quickest by helping others to succeed."*

Though quoted by different people, these proverbs are geared towards one specific topic.

> *"In giving everything you have to others, you'll get more than you can imagine in return."*

I strive to live by this ideal by putting others before myself. Through my life's journey, I have found that I succeeded far more in my goals, and was also happier, when I was helping others. I'm like a river, rather than a reservoir. As I share water with others, I'm replenished by my generosity.

Fulfillment is found by living life focused on others. After all, life's purpose is greater than ourselves. We may not always be able to ignore self-interests, but we should try living for others. Even through our imperfections, the effort is very rewarding.

Praying the Temple Mount Prayer

Lord, Creator and Transformer. You forged me in the warmth of Your grace, fashioned me as an instrument of Your enlightenment and love. I am grateful for Your blessings, Your protection, and Your hope.

Grant me light, that I may fuel the world in Your fire. Grant me patience, that I may serve humbly to bring peace to a world of stubborn violence. Grant me strength, that I may carry those I love on my back when they are tired.

Transform me daily, more and more into a less imperfect reflection of your will. Sharpen my edges that I might slice open little rents into this life, so that others might peek at Heaven.

I give You thanks for what I am, and for what I may become, through You.

Part 2 –
Personal Tributes &
Reflections

A Mom's Sacrifice

No matter how old a man gets, he still misses his mom. My mom passed away 14 years ago, and I certainly miss her.

On Mother's Day, I usually post a tribute to my mom and to all the other exceptional mothers who celebrate this special day. Though I want to recognize them, I also want to reflect a little deeper on what makes our mothers so special.

When I was growing up, my mom was considered a *stay-at-home* or a *non-working mom*. Sometimes, this term brought her regret. Proudly, she would tell my oldest son she would be a meteorologist if she had been born today.

My mom did have a job once as a secretary for the United States Navy in Spain. This was before she met my dad. Once my siblings and I were born, we became her occupation. She chose to focus on making us the measure of her productivity and contribution to the greater society.

I was lucky to have my mom home waiting for us every day from school. She always made sure that we kids arrived home safely and that meals were warm and waiting for us at the dinner table. She pushed us to do well in school and to be kind to others, and she demanded that we make something of ourselves. In doing that, she was as successful as many business people.

Today, I am a doctor. My brother is a well-respected scientist and an executive in a major biotech company, and my sister is a lawyer. Not bad for a woman who wasn't able to go to college and only had a dream of becoming a meteorologist!

Most importantly, my siblings and I are healthy, happy, and motivated citizens and parents ourselves. It's the kind of legacy any career-minded person could be proud of.

Thank you Mom for all your hard work and for the sacrifice you made to make sure we had everything we needed to be successful.

Today, society likes to make a distinction between working moms and stay-at-home moms, as if stay-at-home moms *don't work*. However, motherhood is work no matter whether you decide to step into the business world or stay at home to raise your children. This was my mom's greatest purpose, and she somewhat felt lost after my siblings and I left home. I'm sure the workload was greatly lightened for her.

I want to acknowledge the stay-at-home moms of yesterday and today. Multi-tasking, independent mothers are something to be admired.

Farewell to Abuela

Someone once advised to *write your plans in pencil but God the eraser.*

> *"The Best things in life are nearest: breath in your nose, flowers at your feet, duties at your hand, the path of right just before you. Then do not grasp at the stars but do life's plain, common work as it comes certain that daily duties and daily bread are the sweetest things in life."*

The famous writer, Robert Louis Stevenson, suggested in his writing that the goal of life is not to make millions of dollars or become a famous celebrity but, instead, to take pride in doing what is right and to serve others with the kind of love God calls us to exemplify. It wasn't worldly accolades or personal glory that motivated my grandmother to cook or clean, or lend an intent ear but, instead, it was the faith she had in the power of love, as well as the undying strength she exerted to make sure everyone was taken good care of that drove her –

and no one who has met her can claim any different.

Throughout her life, my grandma enjoyed more than anything to cook for those she loved. Her croquettes after practice or work have become somewhat of a legend in our family, and seemed to be her own kind of medicine. It wasn't that slaving over a stove or the tireless preparation of meals that was so much joy for her, but the thanks and smiles of a well fed friend were more than just, due compensation to her mind.

Her whole life, my grandma was afraid of lightning. She used to tell me stories of how the English nuns, when she was a school girl, would sit her down in front of a large window during a thunderstorm and force her to watch the lightning strikes, in hopes that it would cure her. My grandfather, her husband and a psychiatrist, tried to hypnotize her with the same intent. Needless to say for those of us who knew her, they both failed miserably. Still, she moved to Florida disregarding what she knew to be the daily showers and thunderstorms so closely with our summers here, so that she could be nearer to those she loved most, her family. Every afternoon like clockwork, the thunder would bang, the lightning flashed, and she would retreat to her escape in the closet. She always took her radio, or a load of laundry to fold. Many times over since I was a little boy, I would go too to keep her company. We had many of our best conversations in that dim light, so in a way, you could say I've benefited from her terror. As I think of her now, I can't help but realize beyond my own anguish and sorrow, that she has no fear anymore. She's terrified no longer, and the peace she so desperately summoned here on earth has at least been granted to her.

Back when my grandma was growing up, women didn't have the same opportunities as they do today, and she told me many times that she would have loved to have been a meteorologist if she had gotten the chance. She used to laugh and ask me, "How hard could it be? There's no pressure, everyone expects you to be wrong anyway." She always said she could do a much better job than any of those people on television. I would kid her every time she mentioned it, about how she planned to be a weatherperson when she was so afraid of lightning. She seemed to have her response ever ready, as she informed me of her plan to be able to hide, since, "Hey, she'd know they were coming."

Although my grandmother didn't become a television weatherperson, she was able to accomplish much more. As a mother, she raised a doctor, a biochemist, and a lawyer – who could argue with that? She confided in me many times that she thought her children hated her for always being so vigilant as they were growing up. She joked then about always picking them up from school, and forcing them to bring their friend's parents home so that she could meet them. I think I speak for each of them when I say that they're glad to have had someone like her to look out for them. They may not have admitted it then, but their mother shaped who they have become today by the kindness, caring, and love she had for them, and perhaps that was her greatest accomplishment.

Grandma laughed when recounting how she would have to spank my father when he would fight with my uncle. My dad, she said, scared under the bed, hoping foolishly that the bottom of her slipper wouldn't find him. She regretted having to hit them, but was firm in always defending the way she raised her kids, and she has three wonderful people to present as evidence to that effect.

With her on that journey was my grandfather, Luis. She met him at a naval base in Spain where he was working. She told me that when someone needed a cigarette and there weren't any to be found, she would tell them to go ask *that Mr. Torres over there*, for she always knew he would have some. The other secretaries and office workers didn't think my grandpa to be kind or pleasant enough person to ask for a smoke, but obviously they didn't know him as she soon would. Eventually she proved them wrong. Their love has been one of mutual admiration and compassion. At her husband's bedside through multiple heart operations and stomach ailments, Manoli never tired of caring for him, staying in hospitals till the absolute end of visiting hours, as he did for her in her final days. A Swedish proverb depicted their companionship in saying that *a shared joy is a double joy, and a sorrow is half a sorrow.*

If you are to measure a person by the lives they touch, then my grandmother had a stature taller than any ruler could ever count.

Victor Hugo, the most romantic of French writers, once wrote that *to love another person is to see the face of God.* If this is true, then my grandma is visiting today with an old familiar friend.

Herman Broch, an Austrian novelist, said that *no one's death comes to pass without making some impression, and those close to the deceased inherit part of the liberated soul and become richer in their humaneness.* That saying can be no truer than in what we experience in losing my grandma.

My Abuela Manoli loved mass and frequently proclaimed it as her most prized trip of the week. She never missed church whenever physically possible, and frequently described a Sunday without mass as no Sunday at all. She never missed a single mass while I served in as an altar boy. We cannot ever forget what she taught us here on earth, but we can never stop living it either.

We all can rest easy in knowing my grandma is at her highest and most secure level. The question which ponders us is, "What will life be like without her presence?" Only time will yield a response but, in the meantime, we can show our reverence for the life she led by shaping our own actions to mirror hers. Her legacy is not fixed in any sum of wealth or attached to any earthly possession, but instead her legacy is living and breathing in each of.

> *"To know the road ahead, ask those coming back."*

While we can't sit her down at a table anymore and pose her those questions, we can take from her life the examples she would have given as answers. We can pray for it and she will tell us. Whether it be enjoying an extra mass a year, as she would have, or letting someone pass you in traffic or forgiving someone who does something bad to you, I'd urge you to take from this not only the pain associated with loss, but to reflect on how you too can live as she did – caringly, lovingly, and beautifully.

Elisabeth Kubler-Ross, a former Swiss-American psychiatrist, describes death as *graduation*.

> *"Death is simply a shedding of the physical body, like a butterfly shedding its cocoon. It is a transition to a higher state of consciousness where you can continue to perceive, to understand, to laugh, and to be able to grow."*

The famous American writer, Mark Twain, equated death to a dream when he remarked:

> *"We sometimes congratulate ourselves at the moment of waking up from a troubled dream; it may be so the moment after death."*

If the former is true, my grandma has graduated with honors and is freely enjoying her eternal vacation from the pressures of life.

We often ask at times like these *why*, but a wise man once said:

> *"Submission to God's will is the softest pillow on which to rest. That we should trust God's authority not man's majority."*

As we remember Manuela Torres, let is not dwell on the tragic end of her stay here on earth but, instead, let us focus our attention to the humble way she went about her daily tasks, as a loving mother and devoted wife, and let us take something from that. I have, in my life, spent more time in her company than not, and I will always carry a piece of that with me wherever I go.

She never learned to drive and was dependent on other's taking her where she needed to go. Her face lit up at the news when I told her that I had gotten my driver's license, not even a month ago. She looked forward to rides with me in my car. Unfortunately, she hardly got the chance to enjoy it. Well, from today on she doesn't need a chauffeur, for with God as her guide, she is everywhere watching over us as she did when she was alive.

Every year when I go for my physical, the doctor tells me the story of his uncle John, his moral barometer and compass. He urged me to find someone like that for me when I have to make my own decisions in life. To myself, I knew that my grandma fit the bill. When anything needed discussion I was quick to look for her opinion, I trusted her voice, and I will forever carry her with me as my moral barometer, listening still to the wisdom she undoubtedly has yet to bestow.

Our great love, Manoli, will forever in forms we could never have imagined, lives on. She loved to watch old movies and learn from their lessons, and I can't help but to dream of her meeting all those famous actors and actresses whom she once admired, getting to know them and maybe teaching them something of her own.

She was surrounded at her death by those she loved. Let us pray that she, whom we hold so dear, forever surround our own lives. *~Jordi Torres*

Love for Mom

Wishing my wife a simple *Happy Mother's Day* just wouldn't be enough today. After all, she has many jobs, but my sons – Jordi, Gabriel, Daniel, and Segi – have said it best.

> *"Happy Tutor's Day, Mom, for when you finished a 12-hour work day and spent long nights quizzing us before a big test or crafting an art project with us.*
>
> *"Happy Taxi Driver's Day, Mom, for when you had to drive all four of us to four different locations for sport practices, yet still somehow managed to watch and cheer for each one of us.*
>
> *"Happy Chef's Day, Mom, for always having hot meals prepared for us when we made it home from sport practices.*
>
> *"Happy Mover's Day, Mom, for when you drove or flew with us to college and*

answered the phone when we called you that night missing home.

 "Happy Doctor's Day, Mom, for being our personal physician and helping us through fevers and cold sweats when we got sick a thousand miles away at college.

"Happy Advisor's Day, Mom for giving us advice through tough situations about girlfriends to gainful employment.

"Mom, you were always there no matter what we needed. You dropped anything to attend to our problems big or small. Above all, you did this with loving care and compassion that could only come from a mother.

"So, Happy Mother's Day today and every day. We would not be here without you, and we would not have had the opportunities we've had without you. Relax when you can because tomorrow may bring you a new profession with a new challenge in which we will certainly need you."

Dads are Never Absent

Recently, I found one of my favorite pictures of myself as a kid. I was in Seville, Spain, walking through the city to church with my grandparents and mom. I was clinging to my grandfather's hand, flanked on the other side by my grandmother and mom.

It's easy to imagine the vintage photograph for what's in it. There was my distinguished former Chief of Police grandfather, my determined grandmother, and my mother with her quintessentially 60's haircut in a picturesque medieval cityscape with the church's clergymen following discretely in the background.

However, I realized that the most important thing about this picture might be what can't be seen in it. My dad! He was taking the picture and captured that special moment just for me, but he cut himself out of the frame because somebody had to take the picture.

A couple of years ago, I lost my father. We had a complicated relationship, but I still miss him. Though he can't be seen in this photograph that was taken on Father's Day, I can't help but feel like he is still with me.

In some ways, this photograph makes me feel closer to God, my Heavenly Father. Like my dad, snapping the family photo, God is invisible but always present in my life. This gives me great comfort to know that the most important things in life are sometimes not readily apparent just from eyesight.

I hope that those who has a lost or absent dad of remembers that even he, even in his absence, is still a very important role in life. Death, work, travel, mental illness, and dementia can take him away physically, but these fathers are still with us in our hearts. Their absence can also be a gift at times, like my father taking himself out of the frame to make sure I would have the memory of this photograph forever. Let us celebrate our fathers every day.

Reflections on Dad

Five years ago, my father passed away. Like most things, time has granted me even greater perspective to realize how truly lucky I was to have the dad I did.

The image of my father lying quietly in the intensive care unit is still fresh in my memory. Even more than most days, the image is always so vivid on Father's Day. It reminds me of the things he provided for me, as well as the lessons he taught me and the opportunities he worked hard for – just to make my dreams possible.

My dad gave me my citizenship, as well as a chance to live in the country I love. He exposed me to education and to the life of the mind. He encouraged me to travel and see the world so that I could learn to be sympathetic to people who live under very difficult circumstances. He taught me not to worship money or fame, and he gave me a family support system and siblings to rely on.

Sometimes, dad and I had conflicts. As I remember him lying in that hospital bed, I was also reminded of this. While I don't miss our fights, I am nostalgic for the precious moments we spent together, as well as for the attributes he helped me to develop. Many of the things I enjoy so much in my life now are due, in no small part, because of his influence.

As a father myself, I wonder:

> *"What will my children reflect upon as they sit next to me in my final hours?"*

I am hopeful that my children see that I'm trying to build on what my father gave me, and I hope they build on the things I give them and see past any disagreements or tension we may have had.

Whether it's Father's Day or not, take the time to thank your father for all the things, small or great, he's given you. If he's no longer around, thank him in your heart. And, if you're a father, remember that your children can overcome your mistakes. Know that the good things matter despite any missteps, even after you're gone.

Letter to My Father

Just over five years ago, I sat next to your bed in the Intensive Care Unit. I knew then that tubes and monitors could only promise to tether you to this world a few days longer. You were facing your final days on earth and I was facing you, confronting my own mortality.

You are the reason for much of the good in my life. You were serving as a civilian for the United States Navy when I was born in Spain. You went out of your way to have a birth certificate drawn up and signed by the ambassador of the United States so that I could be born an American citizen, like you.

Before I was born, you had been a world traveler and a student. You had enjoyed a carefree, yet sometimes reckless, existence all in pursuit of new experiences to enjoy and appreciate. However, you decided to settle down, when my brother (Juan) was born, so that my siblings and I could have a father.

93

You gave me a mother with all the love a boy could need. With it, you gave me safety and security and built me a home. You even gave me siblings whom I rely on to this day. You allowed me the freedom to grow and encouraged my success along the way.

As a physician, you taught me the value of caring for others and making a difference in the world. So, I became a doctor too and love it to this day. Like you, I never bowed to money or prestige that came with the title. Thanks for being that example.

We certainly had our differences though we approached the world differently. I found you to be selfish at times. You could even be aloof. You weren't as ambitious as me, and you took your health for granted when I struggled to take control of mine. I must admit that even as you aged, I still harbored resentment, anger, and even hatred at times. I found myself wishing you were different.

One of the things about death is that it often makes us nostalgic. Even the greatest nuanced eulogy, of the most despicable person, dances cheerfully from one beautiful memory to the next while painting the person in rose-colored adjectives of humor, poignancy, and love. Then again, maybe nostalgia is just another word for gratefulness. Perhaps death makes us grateful.

Sitting by your side, Dad, made me grateful. It made me curse those times I wished you were different. I realized that those times were just my own narrow-mindedness rearing its ugly head. You were not a despicable person. Despite our differences, I never once thought that.

Our relationship was difficult at times, and I don't know that I ever learned to fully overcome our differences. It's now been several years since you were in the intensive care unit, and I am truly grateful to you and for you.

Dad, I want to tell you that I love you, and I am proud and grateful for all you have done for me and our family.

When I look back now in my gratefulness, I know that, among other things, I am going to remember you for your infectious smile, your witty and often irreverent sense of humor, and particularly your resolve – especially when you lived life on your own terms.

Even in death, you are a gift. I'll continue to be grateful that you were my dad.

El Abuelo (Grandpa)

When rummaging through some old photographs, I came across a portrait of my grandfather in uniform. He was born at the turn of the 20th century in a small Catalan town in eastern Spain called Benifallet. The photograph reminded me that a commitment to public service runs deep in my family.

El Abuelo joined the Spanish army as a young man, sometime before Spain's civil war. After the war, he served his entire career as a police detective in the city of Seville. Spain has a complicated history, and my grandfather played a complicated role in that history. Regardless, he lived to serve as best as he could, and he chose a public life of helping others.

Gracias, Abuelo, for your service and being an example to our family.

As every generation of my family grows up and grows smarter, I hope we continue to fuel oil our legacy of service.

No Fear of Death

One morning, I woke up to the shocking news that my beloved friend, Heidi, passed away from this life. I met Heidi several years ago when she was in her early 20s. She was bound with hope, excitement, and passion for life. I was several years older but, despite our age difference, we built a profound connection.

We had a symbiotic relationship. She knew how to help me when I didn't know how to ask, and I could quiet her fears before she could express them. In both business and life, we helped each other navigate.

There is one very special moment I shared with Heidi that I will never forget. I was floundering on a project, and I needed advice for one of my yearly calendar shoots. Heidi not only gave me advice, but she took over the project. She selected the right photographer, scoured through stores for the right clothes, and hunted down the best locations for the photoshoot. She even volunteered to fill in as a model. I'll never forget how she gave herself to my project so that I could succeed. Needless to say, the final product of my project was spectacular and it was all due to Heidi.

Heidi was a beautiful soul and a kind friend. I am so fortunate to have all those wonderful pictures as little keepsakes of our time together. When I look at them now, her smile still shines a bright light over me, and I can't help but to feel overcome with joy and gratitude for having known her.

The Bible's Book of Wisdom tells us that God didn't make death. That has always seemed preposterous to me. Didn't God make everything? How could such a ubiquitous occurrence be an oversight? Every living thing dies, including humans. In some places, Scripture blames death on the devil's envy, which ushered the phenomenon into the world.

I think if we circle back, God knew that death was coming. In some ways, He gave it to us because it can be a gift. We fear our own physical death, and we mourn the deaths of those we love. It can shock, anger, and confound us. But, it also reminds us to cherish the times we have with our family and friends. It inspires our hope for another life. It begs our reflection and confirms our very place in the universe. When we deny death or dread it, we lose out on the mystery of creation. To face death is to conquer fear.

When I visited Jerusalem recently, I stopped at a beautiful church called *The Church of the Dormition* in honor of the Blessed Virgin Mary. The dormition is the story of how Mary's earthly life was ended. She fell asleep, peacefully, effortlessly, and untouched by fear. Our death can be peaceful like

Mary's. It can be a brief sleep which opens up into eternity. It can be the expulsion of fear from our lives.

Heidi faced death and has conquered it. She should fear no more. I will miss her dearly, but I trust that I will find her again in another life.

Thank you for being a wonderful friend, Heidi. Sleep now in peace.

Letter from an 11-Year Old

I recently received the following letter from the mother of an 11-year old who saw my before and after pictures on my website:

> *"My son Anthony is so adorable. He says wants to work on his abs before his vacation in Aruba. He said that he wants Dr. T's abs. Can you give him some suggestions?"*

Well, Anthony, you are getting a head start on your health and fitness. I'm very impressed. When I was your age, I was embarrassed to take my shirt off at the beach. I would watch all the other kids enviously from the edge of the shore, and I would never wade into the water because I didn't want anyone to see me. I couldn't see my way out. It took me 30 years to make a change, take control of my health, and stop being embarrassed. You are light years ahead of me, and I am so confident that you can eventually have your own set of six-pack abs.

First things first. Six-pack abs for an 11-year old will require a combination of cardio, strength-training, and healthy eating. You also have to know that highly developed abs require certain hormones that usually don't exist in pre-pubescent boys. If your voice hasn't dropped and you don't have a chest full of hair, this is probably you for now.

Any excess fat on your belly is what will keep you from having that six-pack you're looking for, so you'll need to burn more calories than you consume. That doesn't mean that you need to diet or consume less calories. It does mean that you should be active by running around, swimming, playing sports, jumping rope, riding the bike, hiking, and other things you love to do.

When eating, consider wholefoods that come from each of your daily food groups so you can continue to get your required minerals and vitamins while your body is growing. The majority of your diet should consist of a lot of vegetables, a couple of fruits, lean meats (like beef, turkey, chicken breast, eggs, and fish), as well as good fats (like avocadoes, nuts, and seeds). You should also avoid fast and sugary foods. Also, don't eat late at night.

The main muscles responsible for the six-pack appearance are the rectus abdominis. If you have low body fat, these muscles will be visible. Again, you're probably lacking some of the hormones you need right now to build up your abs to the maximum, but that doesn't mean you're out of luck.

You can still have the abs you want and be in great shape. Right now, you're on the right track in many ways. Setting goals is a great habit to develop, and focusing on maintaining and developing a healthy body is going to reap plenty of dividends as you grow up.

My Eulogy

Tragic events in life have opened my eyes to how fragile life is. It makes me come to the realization that I often refuse to believe that I am not immortal. I often wonder what people would say at my funeral.

Thinking about one's own funeral may seem a little morbid. However, it's not as extreme as it sounds. Many leadership development programs actually utilize this kind of exercise in promoting forward thinking. In fact, I learned a version of it at the Titan Summit in Toronto, Canada, by a leadership coach and motivational speaker, Robin Sharma.

Thinking about one's own eulogy forces the consideration of how he or she would like to be remembered. It makes one ask questions like, "Am I at peace with the choices I've made? What have I neglected in life that I should reconcile?" Perhaps we should asked ourselves what David did in Psalms:

*"Show me, Lord, my life's end and the
number of my days; let me know how
fleeting my life is."*

Stephen Covey similarly entreats us to *begin with
the end in mind.*

Writing my own eulogy has forced me to consider
the impression I've left on people. It's forced me to
evaluate my priorities and goals. I'm reminded by
what's important in life, as well as what I have done
and what is yet to be accomplished. Thinking about
my legacy as *starting with the end in mind*, I am
better able to move forward and appreciate how
fleeting my life is. Following is my eulogy.

> *"No one can say that Francisco failed to
> take advantage of life's abundant gifts. He
> gave himself freely to family, friends, and
> strangers alike. He loved sincerely and
> passionately. He privileged enriching the
> lives of others over enriching himself with
> material pleasures.*
>
> *"In his professional life, Francisco was
> constantly fine-tuning his A-game and
> reevaluating his goals. He tapped into the
> creative sources inside of himself and was
> not afraid of taking chances. He preferred
> appearing sometimes the fool so that he
> could always experience the world on his
> own terms.*
>
> *"By helping others reach their fitness goals,
> he soothed bodies and souls. He achieved
> World Class Athletic Fitness in himself but,
> he also relished sharing his success with*

others. He was happier watching a client, patient, or friend succeed than he was winning the gold on his own. Ultimately, he built value which did not exist in the world before he joined it.

"For his family, Francisco has bequeathed a legacy of ambition, kindness, excellence, and generosity. His children credit him with setting them on the path of greatness. He leaves them with fond memories and important lessons. He made them happy and he enjoyed being made happy by them.

"He was imperfect. And in his imperfection, others found frustration and disappointment at times. He struggled with anger and a tendency to retreat into himself. However, he recognized his imperfections and endeavored tirelessly to address them. In his resolve to become a better man, others found inspiration and hope. They felt empowered by his improvements and his story.

"By the end of his life Francisco made an unbreakable habit of keeping an open mind and shunning prejudice or judgment. He looked for the best in others and, consequently, everyone saw the best in him. Francisco took advantage of life's abundant gifts, and he left the world a richer place than it was before he entered it.

"Death can make us nostalgic. Even the most nuanced eulogy for the most despicable person dances cheerfully from

one beautiful memory to the next, painting
that person in rose-colored adjectives filled
with humor, poignancy, and love.
However, our nostalgia makes us grateful.
Death often makes us grateful."

If I may give any advice, that is you don't have to wait for death to experience our own mortality. Give writing your own eulogy a chance. What will others remark about the legacy you've left behind? Do you need to change course? Re-designate priorities? Where are you weak, and where are you strong? We can't edit our eulogies once we're gone. Don't wait to start working on yours.

Me in Cadiz, Spain

Me & My Brother (Dr. Juan L. Torres)

My Brother, Me, and Mom

Mom, Dad, and Me

Mom & Dad (Manuela Ramos Borrego & Luis A. Torres Vidal)

Mom

Abuelo Ramos, Me, Abuela Candida, and Mom in Seville, Spain

Abuelo Paterno - Dr. Luis Torres Diaz

*Abuela & Abuelo (Candida Borrego &
Juan Ramos Treig*

Abuelo Ramos

116

Abuelo & Abuela in Spain

Abuela, Tía Ana Borrego, Tío Antonio Pozuelo, and Abuelo,

Mom

Mom & Me in Seville, Spain

Me & My Wife (Dr. Elvira Barroso Vicens)

Loss Muchachos (Gabe, Sergi, Jordi, Daniel, and Me)

La Familia (Gabe, Sergi, Daniel, Genzi, Jordi, Elvira, and Me)

My Son (Naval Officer) & Me

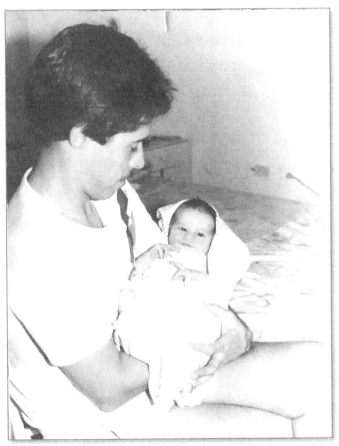

Me & My First Son, Jordi

My Boys (Daniel, Gabe, Sergi, and Jordi)

Jordi & Mr. Walter Cronkite

Abuelo Cono (Don Jose Barroso) & Jordi

My Son (Gabe) & His Dream of the Big Leagues

126

Me (Kiko) & Formula One Car

Arnold Schwarznegger & Me

Me at the Southern Wall of Temple Mount, Jerusalem

Part 3 –
Encouragement towards
Healthy Living

Change Your Mind to Change Your Body

When I was still struggling with my weight several years ago, I often felt anxious as I buttoned up a pair of my jeans. Instantly, I felt apprehensive about how tight they were as they pinched the skin around my waist. The anxiety mounted which turned to disappointment, frustration, and sadness.

For many people, eating is a comforting activity. I too chose this activity for myself once. Sadly, I mollified these feelings with slices of bread from my kitchen's pantry or a trip to McDonalds. These foods are called *comfort foods* for a reason. They certainly gave me comfort – at least temporarily. Often, this choice is made to avoid loneliness, depression, and anxiety. It's a scientifically explainable phenomenon.

Most people desire the *perfect body*. We linger in line at the grocery store, mulling over a magazine cover, and secretly wishing we looked just like the model it displays. Sometimes, we turn to some of the hundreds of books, websites, powders, and pills which offer quick fixes and effortless paths to six-pack abdominals.

I'm here to tell you that there is no lasting magic cure for physical wellbeing. Comfort foods are easy, and long-term health and happiness is not a one-step process.

Somewhat counterintuitively, we don't start slimming down by eating *right* or working out. For many, toning up the legs or abs is first priority, but the first step doesn't involve these. However, it does involve one of the body's organs – the brain.

Fight Negativity with Positivity

Many people think with fairly positive attitudes when starting a new diet or exercise routine.

> *"Gee, I would really like to be healthy again... I need to get off these medications... I want to keep up with my kids... I want to see my grandkids off to college."*

These are the inner strengths needed to keep going, make the right choices, and persevere. Unfortunately, these thoughts don't exist unmolested in one's mind. They are constantly attacked by creeping negativity, and those negative thoughts chip away at the good ones and drive a person away from his or her goals.

> *"This cupcake will make me feel good right now.... I'm too tired to cook after work... One night of unhealthy eating won't be noticed in the morning."*

Banish the negative thoughts which threaten your motivation for losing weight. Always fight negativity with positivity. You may need to convince yourself, but tell yourself positive things over and over again.

> *"I look amazing... I have boundless energy... I love running and working out... I am beautiful."*

See the best version of yourself, the one you're inevitably going to become. Don't let the *now* become your prison. Think about tomorrow for a moment, and even though is not guaranteed, plan for it by being positive about it.

Don't Take Shortcuts

Timesavers won't get you anywhere either. Feeding the mind with *shortcuts* only creates desperation.

> *"I must be thin, so I just won't eat."*

This undermines a healthy, long-term approach to sensible eating.

Starvation is a shortcut that isn't sustainable, and it won't make you the person you want to be. Perfectionism pervades this thinking, but you're already perfect. Conform your choices to that perfect notion of yourself, not the other way around.

Plan for the Long-Term

Sticking to a diet – or anything else that requires determination – may seem very difficult. Allowing this type of thinking can render you helpless. In fact, that is what you're telling yourself when you say that dieting is too hard or you just can't do it. These thoughts are unfortunately self-fulfilling prophecies.

Instead of worrying about the difficulties, focus on the long-term. Celebrate small successes. Make instrumental changes, and don't let yourself get seduced by the lying, fad diet promising immediate results. They will never last.

Battle Sugar Addiction

Sugary foods trigger pleasure centers in the brain. They actually release opioid-like chemicals. Like narcotics, they are addicting. They intensify and expand cravings for similar foods. If you're the type of person who loves sweets, you may need to treat it like an addiction.

Food addiction is something that must be overcome. If you're addicted to sugar, think about reviewing some informative material from *Alcoholics Anonymous*. Though your addiction may be *sugar*, addiction is still addiction and this non-profit organization can be very helpful with this.

Change Your Mind as Therapy

Being overweight can feel awful. For some, it's the worst thing imaginable. It can immobilize you both physically and emotionally. These reactions can be disproportionate. Being overweight doesn't make you the starring figure in a Greek tragedy.

Unfortunately, your struggles are not necessarily unique. Nor are they as insurmountable as they might seem when you're insulated in your own little world. If you're stuck in a pool of self-negativity, perhaps it's time to have the *end-of-days* outlook. Though this may not seem related, changing your mind by thinking of others can be very therapeutic for the brain so that you're not always focused on negative aspects of yourself.

To help recalibrate your self-perception, give back to those less fortunate than yourself. Be generous, and engage in random acts of kindness.

Find Your Self-Worth

Ultimately, this all boils down to feelings of self-worth, as obesity can be viewed as a sign of weakness. Society binds beauty to *being thin*. It's easy to tell yourself that you're not good because you're struggling with your weight, and it's hard to be motivated when you feel this way. These feelings of unworthiness will only make your life miserable.

While health and physical wellbeing are important, so is your *humanity*. It's what makes you the person you are. Though it's worth committing energy to optimizing your biological wellness, you must remember that you are loved for so much more than your waistline. Your mental and spiritual wellbeing is equally, if not more, important.

Your self-worth has to be dependent upon more than just what the scale reads, so stop putting all your eggs in one basket by being consumed about your looks. Channel your strengths to address your weaknesses by focusing on what you do well. Love the good things you already put out into the world.

You'd be surprised how powerful the brain is. Be intentional about your decision to take your wellness into your own hands. Value the long-term successes over the easy fixes. And, share your journey with others as studies prove you are far more likely to succeed if you do. Change your mind in order to change your body, as these things go hand-in-hand.

Learn the Secret to Health

There's no big secret to being healthy. In fact, it's a Mary Poppins style bag full of *little* secrets. You have to learn each one at a time until you've learned them all. Once you do, you'll be on the magical path of a truly healthy lifestyle.

Many people are looking for a magic pill to lose weight and get health. They cling to fad diets and 12-week programs hoping for the model body they've always dreamed of. Unfortunately, most of them don't work. For the ones that do, they are usually not sustainable after a short time.

Changing your lifestyle requires incremental improvements, and these are the little secrets I speak about. You have to be practical and realistic. Little consistent changes can yield massive results. Losing one pound a week means losing 52 pounds a year. For most of us, that is way more than enough.

These small changes can lead to one to three pounds of weight loss in a week, even without changing anything else that you're doing. Stick with them for a minimum of six weeks to let them become a habit. Once you have this down pat, then it's time to change another bad habit.

Secret #1 – Change Your Foods

Write what you eat down on a journal for three days. Afterwards, look it over and find the areas that you can change. This is called *thinking intentionally and monitoring your habits carefully*. You may just find what is holding you back from attaining your goals.

- If you have two slices of regular bread, only eat one slice of Ezekiel bread.

- If you use margarine, trade it out for butter.

- If you drink regular milk, try flax or almond milk.

- If you eat sugary desserts, replace it with berries and nuts.

Secret #2 – Don't Eat Before Bedtime

Most people go to bed by 10 o'clock in the evening. If that's you, try not to eat after 7 o'clock. Never go to bed on a full stomach. By not eating for two to three hours before going to bed saves your metabolism. It also lowers insulin levels and allows your body to burn extra calories.

Fasting for at least 12 hours each night has a positive effect on your metabolism and also creates longevity. If you absolutely have to eat something within this timeframe, eat foods with a little protein and higher in fat such as nuts or natural cheese. This will satiate you throughout the night. Never eat any sugary foods, carbohydrates, or fruit before bedtime.

Secret #3 – Try a Keto Diet

With a ketogenic diet, your body is using fat as an energy source. Otherwise, your body is running off of sugar. It needs to get through all of the sugar before it can even burn fat. You may want to pick up my new book entitled *Keto with a Healthy Twist* to learn just how to do this.

Secret #4 – Perform Cardio Training Early

By doing your cardio training early in the morning, before you eat anything, is more effective at burning body fat. At this time, your glycogen stores are lower than the rest of the day. Therefore, you may be able to burn body fat more efficiently.

Secret #5 – Do Resistance Training

Weight or resistance training is also very effective at burning fat. Many times, it is more effective. In addition, it helps you build and maintain muscle mass. The more muscle you have, the more fat you can burn. No worries, Ladies! You'll never get bulky like men as you only have a very small fraction of testosterone. By doing this type of training, your body will be defined and shapely.

Secret #6 – Get Rest

Getting your rest, including a good night's sleep, is very important for losing weight and getting healthy. Be sure that you're getting at least 7 to 9 hours of restful sleep each night. Menopausal women and those with hormone deficiencies, a little catnap may be needed in the afternoon – even if it's only for five minutes.

Secret #7 – Bask in the Sun

Vitamin Sunshine is extremely important for weight loss and health. Be sure to go outside for at least 20 to 30 minutes every day. For those of you who live in northern regions, you may need to bask in the sun even longer each day to build up for the days you won't get sunshine in the winter.

Secret #8 – Manage Stress

Stress can hang on to weight and also cause many illnesses. It's important to manage your stress. If life's circumstances have gotten you down and you don't know how to get back up, seek out professional help.

Secret #9 – Enjoy Life

Life is short and to be enjoyed. Focus on what's most important in life such as your family and friends. Don't have tunnel vision about any one thing. This can easily happen to people who are focused on weight loss and health. Manage your health daily, but be happy.

Conclusion

As you see, there's no *one big secret* to finding health. Sometimes, you've got to dig deep into your bag of tricks to find the right combination of things that works best for you. Working on one, two, or three small changes can make a huge impact. Be consistent, and you will see results.

Always be Active

Over a decade ago, I was diagnosed with a *bad back*. My doctor insinuated I was doomed after showing me the x-rays and a magnetic resonance imaging (MRI) that he took of my lower spine. Though the calamity of my doctor's words were extreme, it's what many people who have a bad back hear from their doctors.

Since my diagnosis, I thought the days of strenuous physical activity, or running long distances, were a thing of the past. However, I've completed numerous half-marathons and one ultra-marathon. Additionally, I've competed in bodybuilding contests (even won 1st place in one). I continue to run long distances, and I am still active to this date. I have never let my *bad back* stop me, so I suppose my doctor was wrong.

Eight out of 10 Americans will feel back pain over the course of their lives. It is the second most common reason for doctor visits.

Back pain seems to be a mysterious, long-term condition that needs relief. Doctors prescribe special devices, strange exercise plans, medicine, and surgery. Pharmacy shelves are stocked to the brim with expensive back braces and pulls, pain potions, and other gimmicky cures. Have you seen all those television advertisements for special beds to comfort backs?

What's worse is that many people are told they must give up their favorite activities and accept pain as a routine part of life. That's when the cycle begins. Discomfort leads to inactivity, lousy feelings, weight gain, and ultimately more pain.

This is a tragedy because most back and neck pain are simple to predict, prevent, or even reverse. Life isn't over because of a *bad back* diagnoses.

The good news is that back pain is not a standard symptom of aging. Walking upright on two legs didn't create the problem. The problem arose because of lifting something incorrectly one day or because of bad posture, lost arches in the feet, or sitting too long. Inactivity is also a culprit, and bed rest can even make back pain worse.

Back and neck pain usually develop slowly over time, without us even taking note. Just like any bad habit, it can cause trouble over time.

Sudden pain, such as after an accident or fall, was probably brewing from many simple bad habits. The sudden onset is like a heart attack developing over years that suddenly occurred with one more aggravating factor. The key is to identify and modify abusive patterns.

Again, diagnosis of a *bad back* will unfortunately be given to 8 out of 10 people during their lifetimes. If you're one of them, you may be told to scale back on physical activity, and many of you will obey – especially since any form of activity would seem to be aggravating. However, activity is good for you. It gets the oxygen flowing and strengthens muscles. As a pain physician, I encourage you to become more active. That's my answer to diagnosis. It's the ultimate way to stay healthy and happy – even with back pain.

On a side note though, it is imperative that you receive a full medical clearance from a licensed physician before beginning any type of exercise program.

Stop Seeking Magic Cures

Our culture teaches us to desire the *perfect* body, and Hollywood is a primary culprit. Most of us linger in line at the grocery store, mulling over a magazine cover while secretly wishing we looked just like the model or celebrity it portrays.

Unfortunately, marketers push half-witted products on us all the while trafficking in our dream of physical perfection. They often win as we turn to some of the hundreds of books, websites, powders, and pills which offer quick fixes and effortless paths to six-pack abdominals.

I'm here to tell you, there is no lasting magic cure to physical wellbeing. Comfort foods are easy. Long-term health and happiness are not a one-step process. Actors at the Golden Globes ceremony didn't get there overnight, and neither will you. Only the long and winding road gets you where you want to go.

Don't Buy Into Quick Fixes

I'm sure you've seen the cheap contraptions that supposedly help you obtain washboard abdominals. Marketers used to sell them on late night television commercials, as well as full-page ads in Sky Mall magazines. For a one time price of $19.99, who wouldn't want to try it? After all, it was a cheap and easy sell. All you had to do is strap the gadget over your excess belly fat, turn it on, and watch the fat quickly melt away. It was the Holy Grail!

Okay, you might not be as gullible as I was. Believe it or not, I bought one of those things in the early 2000s when I was desperate to look like the guys in the commercials. When I got my fast abs contraption, I strapped it on and turned up the juice. Unsurprisingly, the fat was still there as I looked in the mirror after several weeks of using the thing. There were definitely no washboard abs.

This might seem like an extreme example, but we are all looking for easy fixes all the time. We might not always be buying a crazy machine, but how often do we go on extreme diets? Take the latest fad supplement? Try an unsustainable exercise plan in the hopes that it will get us back on track?

When I bought my fast abs miracle machine, I was desperate, unwilling to put in the gradual effort, and uncompelled to wait and to invest in a long-term solution to my poor health and low self-esteem.

If I can offer you any advice, stay away from the quick fixes. Nothing worth achieving is won overnight. It takes practice. It takes patience. It takes effort. Quick fixes are a myth, like the old snake oil potions con artists would sell on the American Frontier. Don't buy into it. Nothing is a substitute for hard work!

Axe Beliefs that Kill Success

Until 1954, no one thought that a four-minute mile was possible. In fact, doctors in those days said that attempting to do so could break bones and tear ligaments and tendons.

Everyone had accepted the fact that the four-minute mile was an impossibility – everyone except Roger Bannister, who achieved the unimaginable four-minute mile that same year. By accomplishing this, he *crushed* everyone's belief system.

Over the next 16 months, 11 other athletes achieved the four-minute mile. How did that happen? Well, seeing is believing.

I'm going to share with you what I tell some of my clients who are trying to lose weight:

> *"Odds are that you are the biggest obstacle stopping you from achieving the level of success you desire for yourself."*

How? By thinking that you are somehow different, and that your circumstances are unique and more challenging than those who have had the success. I know what you're thinking...

"Easy for you Doc, but..."

I can tell you with total certainty that people everywhere want to get fit, lose weight, have more confidence, and obtain better health. There are plenty of people out there who will gladly pay to lose body fat, get ripped, and have better health – only if they actually believed that this plan is infallible and guaranteed to work all the time.

The founder of the Ford Motor Company, Henry Ford, said it well:

"Whether you think you can or you think you can't, you are right."

What we can achieve is limited only by what we believe. Is today the day you are going to step up and do what you have set out to do for so long?

If you want to be known for something of significance, show proof that you can do what you set out to do and believe in yourself.

Always be passionate about what you do. Don't be afraid to take chances and fully commit yourself to whatever you have decided that you want to accomplish in life. I ask you today to review your belief system and play with it so you can design an exceptional life of no regrets. Believe in what you're doing and make a difference. Oh, and don't forget, work to be happy. You deserve it.

Choose Consciously

What kinds of things do you always do? Do you *always* have a cup of coffee in the mornings? Do you *always* go to the gym in the afternoons? Do you *always* watch television right when you get home from work? Do you *always* eat a bowl of ice cream after dinner? Do you *always* read before bedtime?

We fall into routines subconsciously. It's easy to do the things we've always done because we've always done them. Perhaps they start out consciously, but they end up becoming as second nature to us as blinking or smiling when we're happy. But, the groundbreaking psychiatrist, Carl Jung warned:

> *"Until you make the unconscious conscious, it will direct your life and you will call it fate."*

A few habits are relatively benign such as drinking coffee. One cup of coffee in the morning can actually be good for you. Some habits are positive. For instance, reading before bed is a rewarding alternative to watching television. However, many habits can have very negative effects on life such as pumping your body full of unnecessary sugar before bedtime. Watching television for several hours each day can also dull the brain and suck up valuable time that can, otherwise, be spent productively.

Habits take up a huge part of our day. They also make us who we are in small and big ways. What are your habits? Are you choosing to do things consciously or subconsciously? Do you even realize that you can transform your bad habits into good ones that will alter your life for the better?

Don't let your subconscious habits become your fate. Consciously choose to do the things you *always* do.

Take Responsibility

Once while interviewing a new patient in my office, she made the following comment.

> "Hey Doc. I know I told you that I wanted to drop a few pounds, but do you want to know the real reason I made the appointment to see you?"

"Yes, please," I replied as I waited for her answer.

> "It was one of those emails you regularly send out about motivation, and how the only way to stay motivated is to motivate YOURSELF."

I then replied, "Okay, that's awesome. I'm glad you got something out of it." She continued talking.

> "Yeah, because really, I used to always blame my husband for being out of shape. He always wants to eat out and enjoy some drinks several nights every week, but then I realized that I'm never going to change if I keep blaming him for my state. I mean, if I

155

really want to change, I'll have to start with myself first."

Surprised, I said, "Wow, that's awesome you started thinking that way." My patient then said something profound.

"Yes Doc. I felt like that email gave me a kick under the butt, and after reading it I was like 'Girl, enough is enough, I'm going to start taking care of myself.' So, I'm here."

Needless to say, that conversation totally made my day. This woman was not only very out of shape. She was borderline diabetic and pretty much digging her own grave with a knife and fork. But, then something clicked in her head, and she started taking responsibility for her own circumstances. As a result, she gained control of her destiny.

It wasn't long ago that I learned two formulas that are very practical and simple to use:

"Responsibility is equal to control, and control is equal to responsibility."

This is where it gets important. Only to the degree that you'll accept responsibility over a situation can you actually exert control over it.

For instance, we often feel like we don't have enough hours in the day. We're all busy. However, complaining about *lack of time* will never change your situation. It just won't. It actually prevents you from improving your situation. These thoughts in your head are real and promote a non-productive thought pattern. They are also revealed by your language.

People ask me all the time, "How is business?" I can say, "Business is not good," but I would be out of control if it's not the truth. Even more, there will be nothing I can do about it if I actually believe my response. But, I'm in control if I say, "I didn't do a lot of business this month." By being truthful not only to others, but to myself, I have the opportunity to change my situation.

The lesson to remember is that there is no power in ignoring the truth of a matter. The only way to succeed is by taking 100 percent responsibility for current life situation.

Never Do Nothing

Close your eyes for just a moment and just feel. Then open your eyes so you can finish reading this.

When you closed your eyes, could you feel or sense anything?

I'm guessing you didn't, unless you were in a moving vehicle or got struck by an earthquake. As it turns out, our galaxy is moving towards another galaxy at this very moment. While you might imagine us being just a few inches along that path, we're actually moving about one million miles per hour. Isn't it amazing? Yet, you and I can't sense it.

Our galaxy is sort of like us, especially when we're trying to reach our wellness goals. We exercise and eat a proper diet, but we can't sense that we're making any progress. At times, this can be very frustrating.

In spite of your feelings of frustration, you *are* making significant progress – even in the right direction. You just have to stay in the path. You can achieve all your goals by staying focused and never giving up.

Stop Holding the Wall and Dance

Each year, people from around the world mark each new year by resolving to make significant changes in life. From losing weight or spending more time with family to reading more books or being more patient, these resolutions run the gamut.

As a New Year's resolution one year, I decided to make more of an effort to dance. After all, the health benefits of dancing are numerous. Like all physical activity, dancing keeps your muscles toned, burns fat, and strengthens bones. It can help increase balance and coordination as well, which is important as we age because it provides balance and coordination, while reducing falls and other physical injuries.

As a less obvious health benefit, dancing may decrease the risk for Alzheimer's disease. Studies have shown forgotten memories to be recalled as those with the disease move to the rhythms of music they recognize. This is due to the rise in brain chemicals that encourage the growth of new nerve cells, according to scientists. By requiring certain steps and sequences to be recalled, dancing boosts brain power by improving memory.

If you're someone who fears getting out on the dance floor at parties, let these health benefits encourage you to do so. I understand how anxiety and insecurity can keep one from dancing, but it is actually fun. Plus, it builds confidence and is a fantastic social experience.

So, don't be a wall flower. Whether it's New Year's Eve, or another night, just get out on the dance floor. Your health depends on it.

Stop the Aging Process

There is an undeniable human desire to slow or ultimately stop the aging process. For hundreds of years, scientists and explorers have sought the fountain of youth. They've looked in remote jungles and hidden valleys for it.

Today's explorers are doctors and geneticists. They don't scour the earth and cross oceans to find what they seek. They explore in sterile laboratories, testing biological samples and developing a scientific explanation for the way our bodies mature and ultimately decline.

Have they been more successful than Ponce de Leon, the Spanish explorer of the fifteenth century, who supposedly discovered the fountain of youth? They have, in fact.

Scientists have discovered that we have a 125-year limit on our lifespan. We know that each cell in our body has an *internal* clock ticking down until our time expires. This internal clock is located at the very tip of our chromosomes in a region called the *telomere*.

When cells divide, the telomeres shorten. Unfortunately for humans, telomere length is correlated with aging and death. So, are the ticking clocks in our cells like time bombs we don't know how to diffuse?

The jury is still out to some extent, but we do know that there are steps that can be taken to mitigate the shortening of our telomeres. In fact, there are tests to measure the current length and, at this stage, I think it's a good idea to know where we stand.

Once you have an idea about the length of your telomere, there are scientifically proven lifestyle changes you can undertake to slow the shortening process and access your internal fountain of youth. We can't live forever, but we can certainly live longer and live more abundantly.

Cherish Your Body & Your Wellbeing

Recently, I got to hang out with my 10-year old niece. At one moment in the morning, I noticed she had her phone pointed in my direction. I asked, "Are you taking a picture?" She giggled knowingly, and I was intrigued.

Suddenly, I heard a few electronic chirps coming from the phone and my niece looked surprised. She laughed some more and then brought the iPhone over to show me. She had been using a new app. My nieces and nephews are all prodigious in their pursuit of the latest games and gimmicks on their phones. This one purported to estimate a person's age based on a candid photograph of your face.

My niece was laughing a good deal at my picture after using it with the age prediction app. This was because the app rated me with two different ages. According to the app, my body was 42 years old while my heart – or rather, the caricature of me on my t-shirt – was 29! Could it be?

I was skeptical, so I sought out some proof. I snapped pictures of everyone around me. The app guessed right within a two to five years of error range. Pretty remarkable, I thought. But, what does it mean?

I take care of myself, but I think the phone app captured a lot more than just physical wellbeing. It thought that I was 10 years younger than I am, because I felt youthful, energetic, and optimistic. I'm still looking forward. And, my avatar? It just goes to show that I'm still in my 20s at heart physically and psychologically.

Why worry about chronological age? A happy, healthy, and active octogenarian is much better off than a 20-something who is sedentary and obese. Why do we look to the years on the calendar when our internal clocks matter so much more?

This app might be a little gimmicky, but is also revelatory. Project the age you want to be and that's the age the world, even the cyber world, will see. Find youth in your attitude and treat your body well, so that you too can be young at heart.

If you want to know your true age, don't look at the calendar. The calendar tells you what your chronological age is, but this number may be far from accurate in defining who you are. The age you feel may very well be the most important factor in determining your health, happiness, and longevity.

As an index of aging, chronological age is deeply flawed.

Part 4 –
Motivation for Life &
Business

Live Your Truth

Each new year, people around the world make resolutions for what they are going to do better in the future. Below are five inspirational truths to keep you motivated heading into any new year. Keep them in mind as you make your resolutions.

Truth #1: To create is more difficult than to destroy, but it's also more rewarding.

It's easy to cut people down and diminish what they've built, but something that doesn't exist can't be criticized. So, go ahead and build upon your ideas. Once they're out in the open, the things you care about can be attacked and denied from every direction. This is not a reason to stay on the sidelines!

If you have an idea and it's true and honest and well meaning, go for it. It may not be perfect. You'll never be 100 percent satisfied, and someone will always find a way to critique your work. The most successful people work past outside criticism and their own insecurity. They push through, and they create. Life is about creation.

On the flip side, I'm not saying there is no room for being critical. There's an important place in our culture for critique. Just don't let critique prevent you from creating. If you read a book and think, "I could write something better," then just do it.

Truth #2: You will only achieve something if you believe you're capable of achieving it.

You can't build what you can't imagine. If you don't make a conscious effort to believe you will achieve your goals, there is almost no chance you can achieve them. This takes some faith and confidence, as well as a lot of practice. We are conditioned to be skeptical and cautious. Rewire your brain, move forward, and don't look back.

Truth #3: Little choices are as important as big decisions.

Many of us will resolve to lose weight in the new year. We'll decide that 10 or 20 or 30 pounds is an adequate goal. We'll measure our success against the scale at the end of a few months. That's the wrong approach!

Change or accomplishment requires incremental progress. Think about IKEA. When setting out to build one of their dressers, they don't just provide a picture of the finished outcome. They give step-by-step instructions. If the screws or skip a step is forgotten, the dresser will be lopsided or, worse, entirely useless.

Big results are the final product of thousands of little decisions. Resolve to focus on the small choices you make such as what you eat for lunch... whether or not to spend an extra 10 minutes at the gym... when to go to bed... how much to read... to smile at a passerby... to cut one bad habit out of your life.

It's more effective to concentrate on discrete, manageable tasks. This isn't a *go big or go home* situation. The course of our lives is chartered by millions of almost miniscule corrections one way or the other. You won't notice the results all the time right away, but accomplishments build up.

Pay attention to the small things. They can turn out to be huge!

Truth #4: You matter to other people which is a blessing and a responsibility.

You exist in the world not just as a being who navigates his or her own life. You exist in the lives of others, and you shape their experiences as well.

When you're feeling alone, remember that you're part of the larger human family. Your daily interactions make a difference. You obviously matter to your spouse, your children, your parents, your friends, and your co-workers. Much of their happiness depends on how you treat them. Don't take that responsibility lightly.

You also matter in other's lives. A smile could make a stranger's day. A helping hand up a flight of stairs might be the difference between someone getting hurt and someone staying healthy. The way you interact with others contributes to how well their day goes and, in turn, how well they treat their families and their loved ones.

Be intentional about those interactions. Do something silly to brighten someone else's day. Give a stranger a good story to tell over drinks. Mentor a junior. Make life just a little easier for someone you don't know.

No matter who you are or what you do, if you exist in this world, you make a difference. That's not just something nice to hear to stroke your ego. It's a call to action.

Truth #5: The only thing holding you back is you because you are all you need to succeed.

It's always been tempting to me to blame my setbacks or my limitations on others. My experience isn't unique. We all do this to some extent.

Our future depends on us alone. The world is as favorable or as discouraging as we see it. Be careful to make sure you have given something your all before you move on. Are you unwittingly sacrificing your own happiness or your own success? What are you sacrificing it for?

We stop ourselves from achieving by focusing on negative thoughts. We fall prey to our defeatist attitudes. Look back on the last four truths. There's a lot of room for you to act. You can make meaningful advances in your life if you are willing to believe in yourself, absorb criticism without defining yourself by it, and act in small intentional ways to change yourself and the world around you.

Be true to who you are, but make sure you know who that is. Are you in your current job because you love it or because you don't think you could get the job you would love? You don't need to make rash decisions necessarily to get back on track. Look for the small steps you can take in the right direction and execute them.

You are the key to your own success this year and every year.

Make Your Bed Every Morning

One morning when he was visiting my house for the holidays, I caught my father-in-law making his bed in the guest room. I told him not to worry about it. I offered to make it up myself later. After all, he was a guest. Yet, his response surprised me.

> *"Thanks, but no thanks. I always make the bed in the morning. It's the first task of the day, and it's one I always know I can accomplish. Once you start letting the easy one slip, how can you ever expect to take on the tougher challenges?"*

My father-in-law still has this mentality into his mid-90s!

After hearing this, I started doing a little research of my own about making beds. It turns out that United States Navy Admiral William H. McRaven actually gave the graduates of the Naval Academy class of 2014 this advice:

"If you want to change the world, start off by making your bed."

Scientific studies support the Admiral's experience, as research shows that people who make their bed in the morning are happier and more successful than those who don't. Here are some interesting facts.

- 71% of bed makers consider themselves happy.

- 62% of non-bed-makers are unhappy.

- Bed makers are also more likely to like their jobs, own a home, exercise regularly, and feel well rested.

- Non-bed-makers hate their jobs, rent-apartments, avoid the gym, and wake up tired.

So, the next time you feel rushed or a little lazy in the morning, just remember, making the bed sets you off on the right track for whatever tasks life requires of you the rest of the day. It's your first chance each and every day to win one. The benefits are impressive.

Show a Little Self-Discipline

Sound familiar? Maybe this was your parents' favorite quip when you couldn't concentrate on your homework after school. Maybe you've caught yourself wishing, "If only I had a little more self-discipline...." Maybe someone has told you that your own lack of self-discipline is the reason you haven't achieved the lean, muscular body you have always wanted.

Especially when it comes to health and fitness, many of us have succumbed to the belief that our failures or lack of success stem from a shortage of self-discipline. Could this feeling have overwhelmed us with self-doubt and guilt?

It certainly crippled me when I first began to worry about my own fitness level. After all, the 26th United States President, Teddy Roosevelt, once told us that most anything is possible with self-discipline. If I don't achieve, that must mean I wasn't disciplined enough, right?

What if I told you that the most successful people in our society don't have one ounce more of self-discipline than the least successful?

To many, this would be a grave kind of anathema. I understand this because I found it hard to believe myself. The truth is, Teddy Roosevelt wasn't all wrong because all of us are born with exactly the amount of self-discipline we need to accomplish anything. What distinguishes us, however, is how we are able to harness our self-discipline.

A drifter convinces himself that there is no reason to strive. He tells himself that he should avoid challenges at all costs and that he shouldn't apply to competitive jobs because he won't get them. He tells himself that enjoying life is for other people, and he looks for the bad to the exclusion of the good. He is committed to his frame of mind. He consistently makes the same negative choices, reinforcing the same bad habits or routines.

That is self-discipline. It might not feel disciplined to be lazy, but habits do take discipline – even bad ones.

The good news is that we are all capable of reprogramming our internal operating system to work for us and not against us. The first step is to identify your own limiting beliefs, habits, and behaviors. Try the four steps on the following page to harness your own self-discipline and to create the life of your dreams.

Step #1: Decide on your desired outcome and develop a narrative for why you want to achieve it.

Don't just daydream. Get out your pen and paper. Write down specific goals with details about how you are going to accomplish the individual parts of each and every objective. Explain to yourself your reasons for wanting the things you desire. Why do you want to be healthy? What's your motivation? Are you trying to ease your own anxiety or self-consciousness? Are you trying to run a marathon? Are you trying to live longer for your kids? Your reasons make a difference.

Step #2: Identify at least five limiting beliefs.

What do you tell yourself that prevents you from achieving the goals you just described? You have to be meticulous about analyzing the beliefs or habits which are not consistent with your objective. Not doing is a habit. Avoidance is a habit. Believing that something is too hard will prevent you from accomplishing what you wish for. You want to lose weight, for example but, instead, you get a donut every morning with your co-workers. You tell the story of your grandfather who lived to be 100 eating donuts, drinking, and smoking every day of his life. Then you use this as an excuse for your own poor habits.

Step #3: Select five new beliefs to adopt.

Now that you've identified the negative attitudes that are dragging you in the wrong direction, what might pull you back the other way? Maybe you noted in Step #2 that you don't eat regularly and that this disturbs the proper functioning of your metabolism. A new belief or habit could be that planning meals on Sunday nights is an important part of your weekly routine. Maybe the fact that your grandfather lived to be 100 on a bad diet means you believe that having a healthy lifestyle yourself will lead not only to longevity but to an exceptional quality of life. Because your genes are good, you will tell yourself that working on your health could lead to tremendous results.

Step #4: Commit to your new habits unconditionally.

This isn't a trial run. You have to come to believe in your positive attitudes and plans. They have to become as much a part of your old routines. Once you reach your goals, remember that this is only the beginning. Climbing the mountain is easy compared to building yourself a home, family, and life on the summit. Reinforce your patterns until they seem second nature and effortless. You are the master of your destiny!

Mature & Grow

Personal transformation is a huge part of life. It helps answer the question, "Who am I?" that many people struggle with answering. It's a question, that when left unanswered, can cause many people to take on roles that do not fulfill them in life. Just because one thinks they *should*, doesn't mean they should.

To figure out who you are, you have to make it a priority to find out. It requires change, and once you discover your need to change, the pursuit will provide tremendous joy. If you don't pursue yourself, then you'll be stuck and never grow.

Personally, I had to take responsibility myself to grow and mature. I had to stop blaming authority and my father. Learning to be the captain of my own life, I had to find people to associate with that would encourage me on my journey. That alone made me better.

Always remember that you are a resilient person. No matter how old you are – 10, 30, 50, or 80 years – you can grow and mature.

Think Outside of the Box

If you close your eyes and imagine a crowd of screaming fans at a Lady Gaga concert, I'll bet you aren't picturing a middle-aged Hispanic male doctor to be a part of that crowd. But, I'm here to tell you that I am a huge Lady Gaga fan and for many reasons.

If you don't know Lady Gaga, her real name is Stefani Joanne Angelina Germanotta. She is an American singer, songwriter, and actress who is unique and unconventional in her attire and mannerisms. As a very successful entrepreneur who has sold millions of albums, she fills stadiums and concert halls to capacity everywhere she performs. Plus, she's won countless awards. Gaga is a household name around the globe.

However, Gaga isn't just selling songs, concert tickets, or merchandise. She is selling a *movement*, and that's something we all can stand to learn a little about. If you ever wanted to be an entrepreneur, Gaga is an inspiration worth studying. Following are a few of her great lessons:

Gaga respects the past and, all the while, she embraces the future.

It's common knowledge she draws inspiration from Madonna, but did you know she's also sang duets with Dean Martin? Did you know she is classically trained? She lists Whitney Houston and Cyndi Lauper among her predecessors. In awe of the great singers of the past, Gaga is a woman who understands and studies history.

However, Gaga doesn't let that awe prevent her from forging a bold new path. She takes root in the past, but she blooms into something uniquely forward-looking. In a world where the newest, shiniest toy often obliterates the memory of what came before it, Gaga appeals to our need for newness while preserving the genius of older artists.

Entrepreneurs are always trying to be the newest, shiniest thing. That's how they sell themselves. On the other hand, Gaga shows us how to be better in the future while also reflecting about the past.

Gaga is focused on discreet causes and positive goals.

Whether it's to repeal the *don't-ask-don't-tell* policy or to advocate an end to bullying, Gaga engages fans in more than just her music. Though she's creative with public service, she is civic minded. It may not necessarily be a business decision she's making, but it is certainly good business.

Due to Gaga's passion for creativeness and art, she uses it to help her outreach. She is an exemplary corporate citizen as she inspires action by shocking the conscious. An example would be the time she wore a meat dress that highlighted her distaste for the United States military don't-ask-don't-tell policy. While she doesn't just come right out and tell you her feelings about a topic she feels strongly about, she does make a statement. Perhaps she's trying to tell us to think outside of the box. Then again, maybe she's telling us to get rid of the box so that we begin thinking for ourselves rather than following others.

Gaga capitalizes on her talents and trusts the world with her instincts.

There's no doubt that Gaga is an enormously talented musician. She wrote her first piano ballad at age 13, after playing the piano for 9 years. She isn't defined by marketing and advertising, but she uses it to her advantage – to share her enormous talent to the world.

In business, we can't make something out of nothing. We must find talent while harnessing and deploying it through whatever tools we have at our disposal. No amount of makeup is going to cover up a bad idea. Still yet, Gaga shows us how to build up off of a base of real talent.

Just as Picasso first learned to sketch and paint like the masters before he started changing the art form, Gaga also understands the fundamentals of her craft. Underneath the avant-garde or the finished product, we not only find complexity. We also find innovation.

Gaga doesn't build a fan base. Instead, she builds a culture.

Gaga often refers to her followers as *Little Monsters*. She cultivates loyalty and dedication. She privileges the protection of established fans over the creation of new ones, and she entices people to join her monster club.

By emphasizing how important it is to be part of the world she created, Gaga is no dummy. She is selling herself. Though she makes a ton of money (a net worth of $275 million in 2017), she does more than just produce award-winning art that sells. As she says:

"It has nothing to do with the way I dress or how I sound. It has everything to do with the power of the message."

Live a Life of Purpose

Countless millions are endowed with remarkable talent and ability. Most of them, however, won't ever reach *legendary* status in whatever field they pursue. Why? Because talent alone is not enough.

In order to achieve legendary results, your talent and your ability must be aligned with your purpose. This is what most people lack. For the majority of us, legendary status won't involve a hall-of-fame induction, a Nobel Prize, or a million dollars.

However, we all have the ability to become a legend within our own small spheres of business, community, or family. You don't have to be a legend to leave a legacy, but you do have to leave a legacy in order to be a legend.

I know what you're thinking – *I'm not a legend and neither are you.* Don't be so quick to dismiss the notion. You haven't given your legacy much thought. The day-to-day hustle of your life has gotten in the way. Don't let it. Make the effort. The implications of failing to think about these things are significant.

How long are you going to wait around to get an answer to your life's most important question? In order to achieve success and significance, you aren't only going to need to hone your skills. You're going to have to seek out your purpose and tie these together.

Your purpose is within you and waiting to be revealed. It's a direction you want to go more than anywhere else. Hard work is a given. As the 35th President of the United States, John F. Kennedy, wisely observed:

> *"Efforts and courage are not enough without purpose and direction."*

Not knowing your purpose is like not knowing you've got a tumor. It doesn't hurt today, and it probably won't hurt tomorrow. There will come a time, however, when the permanent damage is done. When the course is irreversible and when nothing hurts anymore.

Robin Sharma, a Canadian writer and motivational speaker, summed it up perfectly when he said:

> *"The purpose of life is a life of purpose."*

Give your legacy a second thought. Where do you want to go? Why aren't you on the road yet?

Give Meaning to Purpose

Recently I found myself with one of my sons discussing his future. Somehow we got to talking about the meaning of success. What would a successful life look like?

I find that people today are experiencing a crisis of purpose and meaning. Up until very recently, I was lost among those people myself. As I was speaking to my son, this old Mark Twain adage came to mind:

> *"The two most important days of your life are the day you are born and the day you find out why."*

I suddenly felt sorry for all those who have not yet lived the second most important day of their lives.

Success has many definitions. It is different things to different people. It means *differently* in different context. It's hard to measure and yet we all seek it out in our own way. It's not always recognized by others. We are almost never certain that we have attained it.

For me, success can only be defined in terms of our own sense of purpose. It must be informed by a keen awareness of goals and an even keener grasp of what significance we are looking for in it. It requires taking a complete and honest interest in life. After all, a life less lived is an opportunity lost, and the road to success runs in many directions but always through a series of opportunities seized.

At many points in our lives, we are handed measures of success. When we are in school, we are told which grades are good and which are bad. There comes a time for everyone, however, when success becomes less clearly defined. We struggle to find purpose and direction, and we experience our crisis of meaning.

Find your meaning. Develop a purpose. You can always change your mind. You don't have to be a legend to leave a legacy, but you do have to have a legacy in order to be a legend.

Your talent and your ability are wasted when you don't channel them into a life of significance – no matter how discrete and local your significance might be. When you have purpose, work has meaning.

Financial freedom is important, but it can't be everything and shouldn't be the only end result of your efforts. Monetary wealth alone won't fulfill you and can lead to an empty existence. Hard work isn't even enough. As the 35th President of the United States, John F. Kennedy, observed:

"Efforts and courage are not enough without purpose and direction."

Give your purpose a second thought. Don't sleepwalk through life with just getting by. Your purpose doesn't have to be fame. You just need direction. Figure out where you want to go and just get going. You're going to enjoy the road a whole lot better when you do.

Transform Your Thoughts

Trying to gain freedom is like trying to bottle sunlight. However, you can be free today in this moment right now. It just depends on how you choose to run your own life.

It's truly amazing the transformations that occur when conscious thought is applied to all unconscious activities done habitually. Once you make a priority to have the life you really want, determination starts to invade your everyday activities – until your dreams become a reality.

Challenge every single thing you do on a daily basis, and re-evaluate them regularly with a clear mind. Ask yourself if it serves you or not, taking nothing for granted and questioning everything. Stop and think. Study and evaluate. Do all of it. Then just DO something with what you discover.

Never stop visualizing your ideal life until it becomes a reality. Enjoy the process. The potential to create anything you've ever wanted is unlimited.

Prepare Your Mind & Body

Long-distance swimmer, Diana Nyad, gained national attention in 1975 when she swam around Manhattan (28 miles) and in 1979 when she swam from North Bimini, The Bahamas to Juno Beach, Florida (102 miles). As Diana grew older, there was one goal that kept eluding her. She wanted to swim 110 miles from Cuba to Florida without using a shark tank. She tried again and again and again.

The distance wasn't what kept Diana from meeting her goals so much as the conditions she faced during her swims. One of her biggest problems was the jellyfish. They would sting her so many times that her face would bloat, and she suffered great physical pain. Other times, she had to be pulled from strong currents.

It wasn't until 2013 when Diana was 64 years young that she accomplished her goal as she became the first person to swim 110 miles from Cuba to Florida without the aid of a shark cage. It was her fifth attempt. She was exhausted but triumphed.

Why did Diana succeed this time? She trained hard and never gave up. Plus, she didn't let anyone tell her that she was *too old* to do it.

She had a great team of professional people to help her reach her goal. If she would have gotten into any trouble or obstacle, her team would have scooped her out of the water instantly.

She also learned from her previous mistakes. This time, she wore a full-body wet suit that protected her from head to toe from the painful jellyfish stings.

Will you dare to be as brave as Diana?

I believe that any of us can be as strong mentally and physically as this great athlete. First of all, you must prepare your mind and body. Never let anyone tell you that you can't achieve your goals and stop speaking negative thoughts of fear and doubt to yourself. Nothing worth achieving is won overnight. It takes practice. It takes patience. It takes effort.

Be an Inspiration

Sometime ago, I was sitting by myself at a medical meeting. I was tired and feeling a little introspective. Then out of the blue, an old friend showed up and sat in the chair next to mine. I hadn't heard from this man for years.

Like me, my friend is from Puerto Rico. We first met when he applied for a fellowship at my medical practice many years ago. We hired him immediately, and he worked under my partners and me for 12 months after finishing his medical residency.

Though a high-achieving doctor, my friend explained to me that he was struggling to find satisfaction in his professional life. After long hours of studying for medical school and a prestigious residency, he did land a good job and worked for a fellowship. Though he enjoyed his work, he didn't know what he was working towards.

My friend hit a plateau in business. He didn't know what his next steps would be. Stagnation was setting in, and he lost his mojo.

To my surprise, my friend told me he had been following my posts on Facebook which helped motivate him. He eventually started his own medical practice and has embraced the adventure. In learning how to manage a practice and grow a business in his area of passion, my friend is moving forward with his life and staying engaged.

Interestingly, my friend told me that he never liked a single thing I ever posted before on social media. Yet, he now uses my motivational posts to enrich his life.

Like him, I hope to reach others with what I share on Facebook and other social media avenues. Though I measure my reach by likes and comments, this proved to me that others that don't engage may actually be inspired. We just never know who's watching, listening, or taking note.

My friends, be an inspiration to others even when you're not sure anyone's paying attention. I couldn't be prouder or more excited about the future of my friend. I'm inspired to know I played even a small role in his success. You too can play a part in reaching others.

> *"Only you can turn a mess into a message... a test into a testimony... a trial into a triumph... a victim into a victory."*

Let Your Passions Inspire

At the start of each year, I try to clean out my home office. After all, 12 months can build up drawers chocked full of coffee-stained notes and crumpled bills. My shredder also gets a workout.

In cleaning out my office, I always run across something I didn't expect to find. Hiding away in a box, I found a copy of my grandfather's poetry book. It wasn't one he liked, but it was one that he actually wrote himself almost 50 years ago.

So this got me thinking...

> *"What was he doing publishing books of poetry?"*

It must have been his hobby. After all, we all have hobbies which keep our passions alive. Reading my grandpa's poems forced me to question how I'm going to keep my own passions alive.

To share a little background about my grandpa, he was a famous pharmacologist in Puerto Rico. He was one of the founders of the original School of Pharmacy, and he also wrote a well-respected book about the history of pharmacology in Puerto Rico. He was an expert in his field.

In spite of his success as a scientist and professor, he was dedicated to his passion. He kept it alive, and I can't help to think that it must have inspired everything he did in his life.

Like Herman Melville who died in a house full of his novel, *Moby-Dick*, my grandpa also died with a garage full of his own fair share of books. In fact, he had boxes full of them.

My grandpa didn't need to write poetry. He didn't do it to pay the bills. He did it because he loved writing. And, who knows! Maybe one day those books may inspire a whole generation. They do inspire me.

Keep your passion alive like writing poetry did for my grandpa. Hobbies may not pay your bills, but they might be just as important as the job you work to pay your bills. At the very least, they'll brighten your day and inspire you to stay sharp and passionate in all aspects of your life. So, keep playing your guitar or paint that beautiful mountainous scenery. Do whatever your passions lead you to do.

Get Out of Your Comfort Zone

If you want to change, you have to be prepared to get uncomfortable. I learned this at an early stage in my life. What I have discovered during my life is that we have to be willing to leave our comfort zones in order to achieve mastery.

In my opinion, pushing beyond the comfort zone forces us to get uncomfortable to make us stronger. At the same time, it helps us recognize our weaknesses so that we can stay on our toes and be in a constant state of vigilance.

We have received powerful tools and it is our responsibility now to use them wisely and never give up while facing the challenges.

> *"A comfort zone is a beautiful place, but nothing ever grows there."*

Create Opportunities

Several years ago, a good friend of mine recommended a thought provoking and inspirational book written by motivational speaker, Robin Sharma called *The Monk Who Sold his Ferrari*.

The story, told as a fable, is meant to be a fun and quick read. I was also impressed that one of my favorite authors, Paulo Coelho, commented about Sharma's book saying:

> *"A captivating story that teaches as it delights."*

Due to the high praise from one of the world's greatest literary figures, I was compelled to read the book. But, what really convinced me to pick it up and read it was because my friend said that it changed the way he approached life forever.

More than a decade later, I read Sharma's fable for a second time, and my friend's recommendation rings as salient as it did back then. We so often ignore the message around us, but thankfully, I paid attention to what my dear friend had to say about this wonderful book and took his advice in reading it.

The plot of the story begins with a successful attorney, Julian Mantle, as he journeys on a search for meaning after suffering a heart attack in the courtroom. Mantle sells his Ferrari and discovers a group of sages (profoundly wise men) in the Himalayas called the Sages of Sivana who help him. Of the group, Yogi Raman adopts Julian as a student and entrusts him with wisdom in which he is to share upon his return home.

Julian finds himself reinvigorated after his time in the mountains, and his experience with the Yogis revives a long-lost sense of purpose in him. When he returns home he shares his vision, as the Sages had instructed, with his new protégé, John. This relationship develops into the main dialogue of the story.

The morality of the book, as exposed in the relationship between Julian and John, is rooted in the *Seven Virtues of Enlightened Life*. Julian reveals each of these, one by one, to his protégé. Overall, the gestalt of the message is:

"The purpose of life is a life of purpose."

Sharma privileges moderation, simplicity, positivity, and goal setting. Through Julian, he proposes simple suggestions for personal improvement. Julian urges self-awareness, happiness over success, ritual, and meditation. He emphasizes the power of passion and the potential of the mind to attract health and happiness.

In the book, the notion of *blueprinting* is introduced. Sharma explains that we create opportunities in the outer world by drafting blueprints in our inner worlds. This is one of the driving metaphors of the fable, and it's become one of the driving forces of my life.

Sharma writes an idea that is earth shattering if you accept it:

> *"Understand once and for all that your mind has the magnetic power to attract all that you desire in your life. If there is lack in your life, it is because there is lack in your thoughts."*

The novel is a love story to human potential. It flirts with the mystic in search of practical approaches to living. It challenges our notions of reality by exploring themes we often ignore in the hustle and bustle of our daily lives.

I encourage you strongly to take some time out of your day and pick up this book. You don't have to sell your Ferrari and move to the Himalayas to reap the rewards of the main character's words. It's a fable to the truest sense of that genre – entertaining and didactic. You'll learn, and you'll enjoy learning.

Every new year, we are confronted with the urge to make resolutions. But resolutions are fleeting. This book explores real mission building. Blueprinting, as Sharma puts it, is about more than the traditional external goals. It's about mindset. It's about finding purpose within and channeling that purpose to achieve happiness out in the world.

Fifteen years later, I'm so glad that my friend first recommended this book, so now I'm recommending it to all of you. This was a message in my life and I hope it can be one in yours.

Let Your Truth Run Loose

Despite what you may think, most truths are not singular. As individuals, we experience truth in diverse ways. Any old truth won't set you free – especially not the ideas inherited from eons of social conditioning and generational pressures. Your own personal truth sets you free as long as you are willing to accept it and embrace it as positive. Here are three basic tips to help you set your own truth free.

TIP #1: Be Transparent

Don't hide yourself from others. In shielding your authentic self from the outside world, you run the risk of forgetting who you are. You can't embrace what you won't let others see. Allowing others to see you for who you are is a benefit for them too. You are nourished by each other's truths, so don't be shy.

Tip #2: Value Your Truth Above All

That sounds arrogant, but it really isn't. It's actually vital. You need to listen to others, and you may think about and absorb their point of view. After all, no person is an island. Criticism can be useful, but – and this is a big BUT – you can't be crippled by others. You get to make the final call by honoring and giving privilege to your own feelings of worth and accomplishment. You need to value your truth above all if you are to succeed.

Tip #3: Accept the Truth

Acknowledging your truth is not about giving up on change. Change, however, takes strength, and inner strength is built on a foundation of self-awareness and self-love. By better acknowledging your strengths and weaknesses, you allow yourself to channel your energies more efficiently. They can change your truth.

In summation, be in tune with your truth. Take time to understand who you are, to accept yourself and to let others see you for who you are – warts and all. If change is needed, build off your acceptance and your self-awareness to channel your energies and have positive, real conversations, and interactions with the outside world. The truth is not singular. We are all our own truths and we need to co-exist. Respect and learn from others, but never let your own truth stay caged and hidden. Set it free, and it will set you free in turn!

Work Smarter, Not Harder

Wouldn't it be nice to work smarter rather than harder? In my opinion, Tim Ferriss' little book entitled *The 4-Hour Work Week* is a must read. The premise of the book revolves around the importance of this sentiment – work smarter and not harder to accomplish goals.

This was such a popular book in the business world that Ferriss went on to create more similarly themed books, including *The 4-Hour Chef* and *The 4-Hour Body*. These also became well regarded, as they taught people that you don't need to spend a lot of time to get great results.

Guess what? This can apply to you too. You don't need to spend a lot of time to get extraordinary results. Dedication and consistency matters more, and excellence can be found if you're truly committed. Just like *The 4-Hour Work Week*, you can do things such as creating systems and delegating tasks whenever possible to free up your time but still get results.

Don't wait until *you're ready* to start writing down your goals and aspirations. That day may never come. Start now and totally commit to a life of purpose and significance.

Escalate Your Return on Effort

The greatest return in life, business, or project is always measured by your effort. It's called *return on effort* or *ROE*. In other words, what you do will give you the greatest return. By focusing on the steps below, you will learn the most important areas to focus on.

Step #1

Create a visual image of what you want your business, life, body, ideas, and goals to look like.

Step #2

Use the resources you already have available, or develop your own resources.

Step #3

Review the areas which you have not thought about, and look for the people and resources you need to have as part of your team to guarantee success.

Step #4

Bring in the 80/20 principle which is about working smarter in anything you do whether it be in life or business. It's about focusing your time and energy on matters that influence your results the most.

This principle was discovered by Vilfredo Federico Damaso Pareto, a lecturer in economics at the University of Lausanne of Switzerland in 1906. He famously observed that just 20 percent of the population in Italy owned 80 percent of the wealth. He then discovered the same dynamics were present in every other country as well. Following are some interesting statistics regarding Pareto's 80/20 Principle:

- 80 percent of any country's population live in just 20 percent of the major cities.

- 80 percent of crimes are committed by just 20 percent of people.

- 80 percent of most people's wardrobes are worn 20 percent of the time.

- 80 percent of Facebook interactions occur with only 20 percent of friends.

- 80 percent of profits come from just 20 percent of products and services sold.

- 80 percent of sales come from 20 percent of your customers.

- 80 percent of business comes from just 20 percent of marketing.

For me, the 20 percent focus will be whatever is the most important or profitable activity at any given time. For you, it may be slightly different.

As you work on this rule, you may find it helpful to write down what your passions are, as well as your strengths. Then work on what will bring the greatest reward or success, and try to harmonize the two.

Conclusion

The key is to know where you can add the most value. Then you'll know where to place your focus and how to manage your strengths and weaknesses.

Maximize Your Potential

It's important to create your own personal philosophies. They will allow you to make better decisions in life, leaving less room for the regretful ones. Maximize your potential by making one or two of the points below a habit. Once you have those down pat, maximize more.

1. Go to bed and get up at the same time seven days per week.

2. Exercise six days per week, even if it's only for five minutes.

3. Eliminate *junk* foods from your house.

4. Choose the two most important tasks to work on before starting your day. Create a to-do list every evening, and start your day with your first two tasks.

5. Don't engage in confrontations with anyone, in person or online.

6. If you have caused harm, apologize. Then try to fix the situation. For any confrontational situation, simply take a deep breath, relax, breath out, and refocus your efforts calmly. Reading Deepak Chopra's *7 Laws of Spiritual Success* can also be a great help. You'll learn that arguing changes nothing. There's no time to let pettiness stand in the way of your main goal of helping others. Life is short, and you must make the best of what you have today. After all, you just have too many important things to accomplish.

7. Take full responsibility for whatever happens to you, good or bad.

8. Accept the consequences of your actions. Don't say, "I didn't know."

9. When you meet someone, sincerely ask them how he or she is doing.

10. Be present and free of distractions at all family and social functions. Learn to put away your smart phone so that you can totally engage with the present moment.

11. Be the answer to someone else's prayer.

12. Don't let negative emotions dominate your day.

13. Be conscious of the temptations, situations, and environments that you must avoid, even if it means losing relationships with who *lives* in those environments.

14. Be honest and trustworthy.

15. Let your Creator and your faith guide your path to become the best person you can possibly be.

Improve Your Strengths

One of the most important advices I ever gave was to my son, Daniel, at the start of his baseball season. I encouraged him to work on and improve his strengths and defensive skills as a catcher, as well as to manage his weaknesses which were hitting the ball and running.

The advice was one I got from one of my most influential personal mentor, Christian Simpson. In the past, I had been frustrated trying to improve areas in my life that I considered not great, such as ballroom dancing.

Though I marginally improved at most of the things I wasn't so good at, I was still only mediocre. Even worse, I was not having fun.

I believe that focusing on strengths is the only way to achieve real excellence. Spending too much time trying to overcome weaknesses often doesn't pay-off enough to justify it. Besides, excellence that comes from working on strengths is much more satisfying and rewarding. This is true according to actor, Tim Roth:

> *"People who... have an opportunity to focus on their strengths every day are six times as likely to be engaged in their jobs and more than three times as likely to report having an excellent quality of life in general."*

Each person's greater room for growth is in the areas of his or her greatest strength. Weaknesses are hard or impossible to develop. Smart individuals learn to manage around their weaknesses.

Work Hard & Give Back

The Austrian-born American bodybuilder, film actor, and politician – Arnold Schwarzenegger – is a controversial figure. He has certainly made his fair share of very public mistakes. That said, I honor him as one of my early mentors.

Growing up in Puerto Rico, I drew a great deal of inspiration from Arnold's success. When I came to the United States many years ago, I obsessed over his work ethics and determination to succeed. Here was a man with an accent – a lot like mine – who starred in movies, was an activist, and sat in California's governor's seat.

His success and his challenge to excel, work hard, and give back were motivational, to say the least. In my mind's eye, I figured I could do these things if he could. No matter his failings, I could still draw inspiration from his lessons. After all, we have all failed in something one point in life.

No one is perfect. Some are even less perfect than others, yet everyone can still learn a few things – even from the weakest among us. And, in honor of them, here are six rules *Arnold style*.

Arnold's 6 Rules for Success

1. Trust yourself.
2. Break the rules, not the law.
3. Don't be afraid to fail.
4. Don't listen to the naysayers.
5. Work your butt off.
6. Always give something back

The day I finally met Arnold in person, I thanked him for helping me accomplish some of my most outrageous goals. We should always thank our mentors.

Stop Being a Prisoner

Consider these wise words from Franklin D. Roosevelt:

> "Men are not prisoners of fate, but only prisoners of their own minds."

He was absolutely right!

When you are looking to achieve some goal, there is no outside force that can hold you back. Fate isn't keeping you from meeting your goals. Strange coincidences and circumstances aren't keeping your goals at bay. As hard as it is to believe sometimes, other people aren't even holding you back – unless you're giving them permission to do so.

The only thing that is standing between you and your goals is your mindset. Are you a prisoner of your mind, or have you broken free of its constraints?

When it comes to regaining your health, your mindset is what will help you succeed each milestone along the way. You can make all the excuses in the world, my friend. Fate is not holding you back from getting the body or health of your dreams. A sick child or parent isn't keeping you down. Your spouse, who wants to sit on the couch eating bonbons during movie night, isn't forcing the same unhealthy habits down your throat.

Your mind can be a powerful thing and can help you succeed in your every desire and dream. Don't let it be the jailhouse holding you as a prisoner.

Learn to Forgive Self

Have you ever noticed that people are willing to forgive just about anything as long as they receive a sincere apology?

A lot of times, people trip over their words and say something to offend someone else. Just think of the celebrity or politician who offends women, ethnic minorities, or some other group of people. If the celebrity or politician sincerely apologizes, the issue usually blows over quickly and is soon forgotten.

Now think about your own life. You probably forgive and forget quite easily with your spouse, children, friends, and other loved ones. But, do you have a difficult time forgiving yourself? Most of us do. Why do we keep beating ourselves up for our own mistakes? Why can't we graciously forgive ourselves and move on after making a mistake?

Be Independent

Independence Day! Has a sort of triumphant ring to it, doesn't it? Each Fourth of July, I set aside a moment to reflect on what exactly it is that we are celebrating in my country. It's the day that the United States of American became independent from Great Britain in 1776.

You've probably read the history books where the American colonies were controlled by Great Britain. The people couldn't worship who they wanted. They couldn't even spend their money how they wanted or decide their own futures. The American forefathers were inhabitants of colonies whose citizens answered to a king across a vast and dangerous ocean.

In 1776, we were given freedom to choose and reinvent ourselves as necessary because of those who came before us. And, we have – over and over again. Over the past 250 years, there have been changes for the worse but, more often, changes for the better. However, we must not take history for granted.

In my field of health and wellness, independence is paramount. It's both a goal and a necessary precondition. Unlike the colonists, we can't declare independence from some unhealthy or sick king. In order to claim independence over our bodies, we must address the realities that are holding us back which are cynicism, bad habits, self-doubt, junk food, laziness, and the status quo.

> *"Are you independent? Do you feel capable of change? Do you feel free to choose? If you think that you have achieved independence, do you feel confident knowing what to do with it? What did you want from independence in the first place?"*

I'm not saying it's easy, but independence takes discipline, sacrifice, and determination. It's hard work to cast off the bonds of tyranny. Just ask the first Presidents of the United States – George, Adam, and Thomas. But, once you have overcome things that have kept you bound, you realize that your goal is more independence, more freedom, and more health.

Independence in my world means freedom from disease. It means the freedom to enjoy the things you love. It means the independence to live a life of purpose and excitement without the constraints or burdens of an unhealthy lifestyle.

Americans are still struggling for independence. Some seek independence from the burden of several extra pounds. Some seek financial independence. Others seek the freedom to love and worship in peace. Still yet, more yearn for an independence of the mind which will free them to imagine the best version of themselves.

Our forefathers struggled so that we could thrive. Don't sit on the sidelines of your own war of independence. Let yourself yearn for personal freedom, and don't be afraid to share your freedom with others.

The revolutionaries of 1776 wanted to create an independent America – they fulfilled their vision. What's your vision? Will you begin to fulfill it today?

Stop Wishing

The opening line to *Their Eyes Were Watching God* by Zora Neale Hurston is:

> *"Ships at a distance have every man's wish on board."*

What a powerful line! How many times have you stood on the *shore* of your dreams, merely looking out at everyone else's ship and wishing you could do the same thing?

Someone else has achieved the goals you want to achieve, so you end up wishing you could do it. But, do you know what happens if you stay on the shore and just wish?

Absolutely nothing! Nada! Zilch!

Wishes don't make your dreams happen. Taking action does. Maybe you're scared to take action, or maybe you don't know where to begin. Whatever you do, just stop sitting on the shore as your wish is on board sailing.

Know What You Want

One of the things that I've learned from my mentors is to use the power of goal setting. By becoming totally immersed and focused on an activity, amazing results can be obtained. However, enjoying the journey completely is important while designing life's goals.

English songwriter and co-founder of the Beatles, John Lennon, once said:

> *"Life is what happens while you are busy making other plans."*

Unfortunately, most people give up on their goals just before something big and wonderful is coming to them. Therefore, they miss the opportunity for precious rewards.

Giving up is not an option for success. We must work without hesitation toward achieving success, happiness, abundance, and a feeling worthiness. By taking control of our internal strength, we can reach our ultimate physical, financial, emotional, and spiritual goals.

Alexander Graham Bell – a Scottish-born scientist, inventor, and innovator – described success very well when he said:

> *"What this power is, I cannot say. All I know is that it exists... and it becomes available only when you are in that state of mind in which you know exactly what you want... and are fully determined not to quit until you get it."*

In order to achieve success, you must first set worthy and achievable goals. Then you must become totally immersed in the activity while avoiding distractions.

Pay close attention to what is happening around you by living only in the present moment and finally learn how to enjoy the immediate experience. Remember not to worry about the past, and don't feel intimidated about the future.

I'm excited about taking my life to the next level by understanding clearly that the external world is not my driving force. I hope you are too.

Stay Centered

It's crazy how time flies! Before you know it, half the year has already passed. Yet, the center can be a place of strength – like the superior game player who plays *center* in most sports.

However, there is a big difference between *being self-centered* and *being centered*. The former involves a constant state of dissatisfaction, while the latter represents a far more peaceful, harmonious, and balanced state.

Are you centered?

If not, this place can help you succeed in accomplishing your goals. You just need to keep yourself on the right track and push forward even harder – just like the *big man* on the basketball court.

Don't be stuck in the middle of a project or your goals. Take the time to make them succeed. How can you make them significant? At the same time, how can you accomplish them while staying centered?

Always remind yourself of the *big picture*. Aim for a life of significance, health, energy, positivity, and satisfaction. Whatever unhappiness you may feel, channel it to accomplish your goals. Stay centered, and follow your instincts to make everything in your life better.

Decide Where You're Going

Keeping *outcome* in mind is necessary for achievement. Every single person, who has experienced major success in my wellness program, knew exactly what they wanted to accomplish and why. Even if they needed a little help finding the right path to get there, they knew where they were going.

Unfortunately, most people don't know what they want. Even worse, some do nothing about it. Those people sit and wait and say things like, *"Someday, I'll...."* But, someday is today. It is right here, right now.

The American entrepreneur and life coach, Tony Robbins, once said:

> *"The road to someday leads to a town called Nowhere."*

Ouch! That's definitely not a place anyone wants to live. So, you might ask, "What can I do?" The answer starts with one word:

"Decision."

You must decide! You might not know this, but the word *decision* is derived from a Latin word which means *to cut off from.* When you decide, you cut off all other possibilities. Still yet, you must stay flexible. Tony is a wise man.

> *"Stay committed to your decisions, but stay flexible in your approach."*

Knowing where you want to go involves deciding what you want and cutting yourself off from failure. Plus, you'll have to decide to not settle for what you already have. By seeing your desired outcome, you won't be distracted or tempted to give up. With your commitment to get there, you won't be able to go anywhere else.

Long ago, I decided to get my own physical, mental, emotional, and spiritual wellness under control. At first, I wasn't very clear about my goals. After I targeted my efforts, I cut off the alternatives and committed to my goals. My results improved dramatically, and I was able to enjoy success. If I have one word of advice:

> *"Be specific. Be hopeful. Work hard."*

Try Being Non-Resistant

The Holy Bible is full of promises. We might say that expectancy is the substance of the things hoped for. On the other hand, expectancy can be the substance of the things man fear.

"The things I expected has come upon me."

Spiritual development is the ability to stand still, or stand aside, and let infinite intelligence lift your burdens and fight your battles. When the burden of resentment is lifted, you experience a sense of relief. You have a *kind* feeling for everyone, which sets in motion the proper function of all the organs in your body.

A clipping quote by the late American politician, Albert Day, reads:

> *"... loving our enemies is good for our spiritual health is widely known and accepted. But that negation and poisonous emotions destroy physical health is a relatively new discovery. The problem of*

239

health is often an emotional one. Wrong emotions entertained and repeated are potent causes of illness. When the preacher talks about loving your enemies, the man on the street is apt to dismiss the idea as unendurable and pious. But the fact is, the preacher is telling you something which is one of the first laws of hygiene, as well as ethics. No man even for his body's sake can afford to indulge in hatred. It is like repeated doses of poison. When you are urged to get rid of fear, you are not listening to a moon-struck idealist; rather you are hearing counsel that is as significant for health and advice about diet."

We hear so much about a balanced diet, but you can't digest what you eat without a balanced mind – calories or no calories.

Non-resistance is an art. When acquired, the world is yours. So many people are trying to force situations, but lasting good will never come through forcing personal will.

Your big opportunity and big success usually slide in when you least expect it. You have to let go long enough for the great law of attraction to operate. You've never seen a worried and anxious magnet. It stands up straight and hasn't a care in the world because it knows the needles can't help jump to it. The things we rightly desire come to pass when we have taken the clutch off.

Do not let your heart's desire become a heart's disease. You are completely demagnetized when you desire something too intensely. This creates worry, fear, and agonizing feelings which become an occult law of indifference:

"None of these things move me."

Walt Disney's fictional character, Aladdin, and his wonderful lamp are the out-picturing of the word. Aladdin rubbed the lamp and all his desires came to pass. Your word is your lamp. Words and thoughts are a form of radioactivity and do not return void. As a scientist once said that words are clothed in light, you are continually reaping the fruits of your words.

Don't Miss Your Opportunity

I was once part of a discussion group where a member told a very interesting story that made me think about missing opportunities.

The story told about a man who had once managed to ride a train entirely across a few counties without paying for his ticket. Because of this, he felt a sense of accomplishment as he disembarked the train on his last stop. That is, until he was caught.

As he exited the station, a non-uniformed police officer jerked him aside. Instead of charging him with just a minor fine, the officer wrote him up for a hefty charge – including a precondition with a threat of a criminal record. The poor man's life could be irreparably damaged.

The man earnestly asked the officer why they had come down on him so hard. After all, he was just dodging the cheap train fare. The officer's reply was unexpected.

The officer said that it wasn't the *cheap free ride* he was guilty of, as much as he had plenty of opportunities throughout his travel to pay for the fare. After all, the train conductor passed him up and down the aisle several times. Plus, he had walked past ticket booths both coming and going. In total, the man had foregone 10 different opportunities to pay for his train fare. His failure to pay each time was what was damning him.

As I was listening to the story, I felt awful for the man. However, it encouraged me to consider all opportunities I've had myself to correct my own poor decision. I began cataloguing the times I've said:

"Next time... tomorrow... next week."

We are all faced with choices to do the right thing every day. Making a mistake once may be pardonable, and making a few mistakes might not even be all that bad. However, making the same mistake over and over again makes us morally culpable – just like the man on the train.

Do you keep putting things off? Do you even recognize when you're turning down the same option multiple times? I challenge you to consider whether or not you are taking advantage of all of life's opportunities to do the right thing.

Grow by Being Flexible

I spent last night watching the movie *Rush*. Apart from the fact that I have been a huge Formula 1 (F1) racing fan since I was a kid, I've been wanting to watch this film for ages. It didn't disappoint.

As a work of art, the movie is exhilarating. It explores the legendary rivalry between Niki Lauda and James Hunt, two gifted F1 racers. The two men push each other to their physical, psychological, and emotional limits on a quest to win the Grand Prix. The movie demonstrates that there is no shortcut to victory and very little, if any, margin for error at the highest levels of the sport.

We can learn so much from the clash between these two athletes, and make no mistake as these guys *are* athletes. There's a lesson in their differences, particularly of their views on risk.

Lauda was analytical in his approach. He carefully balanced risk against reward. He charted these calculations in his mind and he never exceeded his predetermined risk threshold. He was risk-adverse or, I should say, he was as risk-averse as any F1 driver can be.

Hunt, on the other hand, focused singularly on his goals. Risk didn't factor in. He was ready to take whatever risk was necessary to achieve his desired outcome.

Well established Fortune 500 companies and premier consulting firms have been employing sophisticated risk management techniques for years. These companies always choose to be analytical about the risks they take.

New companies don't start out with analysis and risk-management formulas. How far will a new entrepreneur go to achieve his dreams? Often, at the seminal stages, there is no board of directors to constrain the founder or the chief executive officer (CEO) of a nascent company.

In the world of entrepreneurship, the analogy to Lauda and Hunt is an interesting one. Is it better to be like Lauda or like Hunt? If you take a risk, are you taking it purposefully? Should you take risks just for the sake of being risky?

These questions can apply to your personal life as well. At what point do you say no to re-mortgage your home? When do you choose to quit your job and start fresh? How do you decide to end a relationship or to commit to one?

Be different, each of us uses our own risk-reward calculator. Over time, the internal formulas change. Circumstances require flexibility and growth. In order to manage the risks we take in our lives and reach our full potential, we ultimately have to be mindful like Lauda always but also willing to be fearless like Hunt always.

Even if you aren't as big of an F1 fan, watch the movie. You just might learn something.

Read to Learn

Did you know that reading activates your brain in ways that movies and television simply cannot? By choosing not to read, one is choosing a life with less imagination and deep thinking and a more stunted ability to communicate. Consider these facts about Americans when it comes to reading.

- 33% of high schoolers never read a book after graduation.

- 42% of college graduates never read a book after graduation.

- 70% of adults have not been in a bookstore in the last five years.

- 80% of families didn't buy or read a book in the last year.

    The American fantasy and horror author, Ray Bradbury, once elicited:

"You don't have to burn books to destroy a culture. You just have to get people to stop reading them."

Sad but true! This is where the United States is headed as Americans become more illiterate. We're already starting to see the negative results.

If you want to be successful if life, go to the bookstore or buy a book online. However, consider what you read as well as this is very important. Following are some suggestions. This is a list of my favorite 25 books. They will help you grow and mature.

1. *Think and Grow Rich* by Napoleon Hill

2. *As a Man Thinks* by James Allen

3. *Mastery* by Robert Green

4. *The War of Art* by Steven Pressfield

5. *The Alchemist* by Paulo Coehlo

6. *How to Win Friends and Influence People* by Dale Carnegie

7. *Flow* by Mihaly Csikszentmihalyi

8. *Richest Man in Babylon* by George Samuel Clason

9. *The Master Key System* by Charles F. Haanel

10. *Man's Search for Meaning* by Viktor Frankl

Channel Perseverance

Most of us set out to be successful. In our efforts, we are told repeatedly that success requires sacrifice and that nothing in this world is free. But how often do we ask ourselves:

> *"What am I willing to sacrifice for my success? What price would I pay?"*

I began thinking more deeply about these questions after watching a penetrating movie titled *Whiplash*. The film follows a talented student at a New York City music academy and catalogues his relationship with a domineering instructor. The student dreams of becoming a legendary jazz drummer, and his vocation completely consumes him. I won't reveal too much of the plot but, overall, the movie beautifully portrays the power of ambition. However, it also reveals the steep price that success sometimes demands. The tagline of the film is befitting:

"The road to greatness can take you to the edge."

You may have also heard that talent alone is worthless without drive and determination. That drive and determination, in turn, leads to success only when it is focused. But, what is too much focus? When does it hamper success?

In *Whiplash*, the drummer boasts that he has no friends. He dumps his girlfriend in order to devote himself completely to his passion. More than one psychiatrist or psychologist will tell you that this isn't a healthy approach, but is that what's required to achieve greatness? A famous English writer, Samuel Johnson, once wrote:

"To be unhappy at home is the ultimate result of all ambition."

Can that be right? Success at the highest level sometimes requires a certain amount of monomania. The road to success might or might not lead you to the edge, but it is doubtlessly lined with obstacles and repeated failures. The only way to make it to the end is to persevere, and perseverance doesn't allow for much equivocation or compromise.

Never fear though! There are ways not to lose yourself in the quest for success. The key is channeling your perseverance and keeping your focus resolved. Setting concrete goals and tasks is essential. Give your all in stretches. Your success is much more like an epic journey than some sort of prolonged sprint.

Live with some urgency, but take time out to rest between milestones. It sounds cliché, but you have to appreciate the voyage. Otherwise, the destination won't be satisfying when you arrive. Be decisive about your plans and honest about your timelines. Most of all, persevere like an uncompromising maniac in the face of failures and setbacks.

Take Action

Think about the biggest tragedies that have happened in the United States of America in the first few decades starting at the end of the 20th century. There was the Oklahoma bombing of 1995, the World Trade Center tragedy of 2001, Hurricane Katrina of 2005, and a several more which included mass shootings.

I'm sure you can remember watching footage of those events and feeling profound emotions. As time elapsed, news sources reported less and less on each story. Honestly, how often do you think about these events today – especially since you're not getting daily reminders of them?

The reason I bring this up...

These are illustrations of how important events can be forgotten quickly. Out of sight, out of mind! If we don't get reminders, we soon forget.

The same is true of the important events and goals in your life. When you first decide to do something, you constantly think of it. If you don't take action, time goes by and you forget. Without daily reminders, you start to think about it less and less. Your enthusiasm may start to fade and your drive, and motivation start to diminish.

Don't allow this to happen. There's a reason why you thought of doing that *something* in the first place. Don't let it escape your mind. Start doing!

Just Do It

If you acknowledge the fact that you create each moment and experience, and realize that your very own experience in life is determined by exactly what you think and feel, and generation can take place from that experience regardless of whether you take control of those thoughts and feelings or not – then creation can take place.

The question then is, "What does the feeling of wanting something create in your experience." The answer is, "You create precisely the very thing that your belief system is consumed with."

It is sometimes not so obvious how those beliefs generate your experience. If you feel deeply that your life is a terrible mess, what will your daily experience be? A very convincing mess, and it will be very difficult for you to see how it could be any different.

If you feel deeply that life is breathtaking, awe inspiring, abundant, beautiful and full of opportunities and love, this outlook will create happiness in your life and will cause you to thrive. It will be difficult to understand how anyone could not see this clearly.

Now, I don't own a pair of rose-tinted glasses. I can see as well as anyone the not so good and indeed terrible things that occur both in my world and globally.

The world experience is a consequence of human thinking and feeling. If everyone changed their minds to reflect the wonders of life, I believe the whole worldwide experience would instantly improve.

It doesn't even have to be everyone that makes that change – just the leaders of the world would do the trick. The people on this earth who are successful are successful because success began inside of them. The outside just had to catch up.

Stop wanting, needing, or hoping. Start being the very source of the experience you desire. The force and the source to create the experience is already within you. As Yoda once said,

"Do, or do not. There is no try."

Many people will quit just before they achieve their goal, almost as if they've pre-programmed themselves to be okay with it. And, they have! If you look at a goal and think, "I'll try," you predispose yourself to being okay with quitting.

Today I want to share four great mental tricks to get you beyond just trying:

Trick #1

FEEL big... dream big... but focus small and take action only on what you can see directly in front of you. Say to yourself, "I'll do one thing at a time and take one step at a time until I achieve this. It will be fun!"

Trick #2

Think of the fun you will have in the process and let go of the result. Great athletes are well trained in this, and you must be too. Tell yourself to simply go out there, do the best you can, and HAVE FUN above else. It's almost inevitably when the athlete who cracks under immense pressure to succeed, who is so uptight and tense, fails to perform at a higher level. The underdog, who doesn't feel the same pressure, plays with a joyful spirit and nails the performance and wins the gold. Don't let yourself feel the pressure by focusing on letting go.

Trick #3

Play with "What if it *does* work? What if, in spite of all predictions, it actually works? Wouldn't that be fun?" Pretend! Mentally rehearse success, but also mentally rehearse the awesomely fun, playful process that will lead to the success you envision.

Trick #4

Tell yourself, "Just do it!" So what if you don't get the results you anticipated. As the hockey player and National Hockey League Hall of Famer, Wayne Gretzky, famously said:

"You miss 100% of the shots you didn't take."

And did the great one *try* to score a goal? No. He just took the shot. He just *did*.

Conclusion

Think about the times you have tried too hard to impress someone you liked, or to give the winning performance, or to hurry the process because you didn't have enough control. What were your results? Did they meet your expectations? I'm guessing probably not.

So next time, remember the words of legendary Star Wars Jedi Master, Yoda:

"Try not. Do, or do not. There is no try."

Thanks, Yoda.

Stay Strong & Committed

Do your goals ever feel out of reach? Now is the perfect time to take a good look at your situation and ask, "Why not?" United States Senator Robert Kennedy once said:

> *"Some men see what it is and ask 'Why?' I see what might be and ask 'Why not?'"*

There is nothing stopping you except yourself. Every day, people just like you and me are successfully achieving their goals. These same people may have felt, at some point, like their own goals were out of reach when they first started.

However, the problem with most people reaching their goals is that they have no plan with specific action steps. I understand the difficulty of putting a plan together and committing to its execution. Amelia Earhart, the American aviation pioneer, made this clear:

> *"The most difficult thing is the decision to act, the rest is merely tenacity."*

Stay strong and unconditionally committed.

Let Anger be a Blessing

I get angry. I get angry in the car when a careless driver swerves into the lane ahead of me. I get angry when my employees and my colleagues aren't working hard. I even get angry when the family dog wakes me up unwittingly from a nap by jumping up onto the bed.

Feelings are truth though. They're the physical expressions of what motivates us. They give us the spark we need to act with creativity and with passion. As Trinidadian-born American actress, Lorraine Toussaint, once said:

> *"We all have a dark side. Most of us go through life avoiding direct confrontation with that aspect of ourselves, which I call the shadow self. There's a reason why. It carries a great deal of energy."*

Anger, like all emotions, can be a blessing. Anger which is destructively channeled leads to very negative consequences. Anger which is left festering below the surface trickles up to infect our mood and our behavior in unhelpful ways. One of the opposites of emotion, however, is apathy. Apathy is as negative as badly channeled anger.

Self-awareness requires recognizing anger. It requires appreciating the fact that the blood boiling in your veins is a sign of life or an inspiration. Sometimes it's misplaced. Sometimes it is the result of jealousy or vanity. It is always, however, a sign that we are alive and that we are moving toward something. Channel your anger into productive energy. Don't let it become something destructive. Don't let it hold you hostage.

Anger is a blessing in the way that all emotions are a blessing. Anger reminds you that you care. If you're able to use that motivation to make a positive change in the world, then anger can definitely be a blessing.

Consider the Hourglass

In 1944, Reverend Dr. James Gordon Gilkey challenged his readers to consider the hourglass.

> *"The grains of sand dropping one by one...
> the crowded hours come to you always one
> moment at a time."*

When you feel overwhelmed by life's challenges, consider the hourglass. Imagine one on your desk at work or on your coffee table at home. Only a single, solitary grain can pass through it at a time.

No matter how busy or overwhelmed you are, or how many things your day throws at you, life is the same. You can only handle one problem at a time... conquer one challenge at a time.

By considering the hourglass, you will gain emotional poise.

Start Fresh

Have you ever failed at something?

Silly question, right? Of course, we all have. I bet every single one of us has set out to do something with big plans in mind at one time or another, only to fail. Whatever our goal, it just didn't quite turn out the way we hoped. Something tripped us up. Either we made a mistake, or we encountered an obstacle we felt we couldn't quite overcome. In the midst of it all, our minds can sometimes be cruel.

> *"If you didn't do it perfectly now, then tomorrow won't be any better. You need to just give up. You're not good enough."*

Important quests in life can unfortunately bring discouragement. It's just bound to happen, but you must remember that you're not alone when this occurs. Everybody experiences defeat at some point, but that doesn't mean we should give up. Lucy Maud Montgomery, author of the famous *Anne of Green Gables* author series, encourages us:

"Tomorrow is fresh, with no mistakes in it."

Life is a journey, each one of us learning every day as we travel our path. You always have to put yesterday's failures behind you, and remember that each day is a new day that can make your goals a reality.

Find Your Ultimate Reward

The leading English art critic of the Victorian era, John Ruskin, once said:

> *"The highest reward for man's toil is not what he gets for it, but what he becomes by it."*

Pause for a moment. When you work hard to achieve your goal, meeting the goal is only part of the reward. The ultimate reward is how it changes you.

Suddenly you find an internal strength that you didn't know you had. You begin looking around your life, taking inventory, and wondering what else you can change. You start to believe in yourself. You become more confident.

When it comes to building a healthy and a meaningful lifestyle, you will reach your goals through hard work and worthy achievements along the way. You'll feel amazing both mentally and spiritually – not a bad reward for your efforts.

Your newfound self-confidence will encourage you to continue. After all, there's nothing more rewarding than feeling proud of yourself for what you have accomplished.

However, the greatest reward is how it changes you. You suddenly discover new things within yourself such as passion, a sense of purpose, and a strong desire to help others. When you feel good and worthy, nothing can become between you and your purpose.

You'll want to share your story with others and, hopefully, transform their lives as well. You make time for people in ways you never did before, and those relationships become rewarding in and of themselves.

These changes make you whole and fulfilled – the most beautiful gift you can give yourself.

Never Give Up

In 2011, a pro golfer by the name of Kevin Na broke a PGA record at the Valero Texan Open. Unfortunately, it probably wasn't the record he was hoping for.

It turns out that Na took 20 minutes to shoot a 16 on a par-four hole. I don't know a lot about golf, but I can only imagine that that's a long time. An embarrassingly long time! It's probably something he probably wouldn't brag about to his golf buddies.

But, guess what? Keenly aware that the media and onlookers were watching his every move, Na kept playing and didn't give up. Even though he must have felt terribly embarrassed, he amazingly kept going. Not just on that hole but with his entire career!

When it comes your own personal growth, do you find yourself giving up easily? Learn from Na and pull out the strong man or woman in you.

Don't let the opinions of others, or even your own fear of embarrassment stop you. You'll never reach your goals if you're worried about petty things like this.

Decide Today

When I was remodeling my office, I decided to hang some motivational quotes on my walls. I searched, sorted, and scoured the internet for the very best motivational quotes. Along the way I came across a quote from one of my early mentors, Anthony Robbins, who is a famous life coach. It's an encouraging quote on how important it is to always know where you're going and what you want.

This theory really resonated with me because every single person that has had major success in my wellness program knew exactly *what* they wanted to accomplish, as well as *why*. They didn't just come in whenever and did what *they* wanted. Instead, they came in with determination to do what I coached them to do so they could reach their goals. Because they knew what they wanted, they also reached their goals easily. Success comes when you first know what you want. The rest is just working for it.

Unfortunately, most people in life have no idea what they want. Even worse is when people *do* know what they want, yet they do nothing about it. They sit and wait while saying things like:

> *"Someday, I'll do this..."*

What they need to realize is:

> *"Someday is now, and someday is here. It's right in front of you."*

Tony once said:

> *"The road to someday leads to a town called nowhere..."*

That's just not a place you want to be in. If you want something, then take action. If you're asking *how*, then here's the answer.

> *"You decide."*

Make a decision to *never* settle for anything less than you can be. Decide to stop living the way you are now, no matter how good it may seem. Demanding more from yourself – more than anyone else could demand from you – is true power.

Live in the "Right Now"

I want to share with you something interesting that happened to me some time ago. While watching my son, Daniel, play an important baseball game, I did something terribly stupid. The odds are, you've probably done it yourself. It is something we all should try to limit in our lives. What I did was... check my smart phone.

Now this may not seem like a big deal at first, but let me explain. I checked my phone to login into Facebook at the same exact moment my son (a catcher) threw a runner out at first with a perfect throw (no instant replay in the Minors).

The tragedy was that I checked my phone on a very important day in my son's life. The mistake was that I mixed work and play together.

In a split second, I realized that I had become a screen sucker!

I, like many others, can't avoid the curse of checking the phone every five minutes. On one hand, we have the world available to us at our fingertips. On the other hand, it totally derails us from what really matters in life. One of the requirements in getting things done right is to *focus* and you just can't do that when you're on Facebook, Instagram, Candy Crush, or anything else.

Checking my phone has intruded into other areas of my life as well – such as fitness. I have found myself checking my phone while working out. I might as well have written on my fitness goals list, "I don't care about results. My exercise routine has become side lunges, Facebook, burpees, text messages, shoulder presses, emails, and then cool down."

You definitely can't expect to get killer definition in your arms if you're on Facebook and triceps at the same time. Can you imagine the great American football player, Marshawn Lynch, checking his phone while running toward the end zone?

We need to be conscious to never, ever mix work and play together. Your work is too serious to play around with, and your play is too valuable to dilute it with work.

The only time you will ever have in your life is the *present* moment. The past is what happened, and the future is yet to come. It depends on what we do right now, and it's really all you'll ever have in life – nothing more and nothing less.

So whatever you do today, focus on being present and enjoy the moment.

Be an Eternal Optimist

When did optimism become an insult? What is it about our culture that privileges the cynic?

I've been criticized my entire life for being an *eternal optimist*. I started describing myself to others this way. Even if I didn't treat the term negatively, it became perfunctory. I applied it like you would the physical traits: tall, thin, blue-eyed. Only recently have I discovered what it actually means that people see me as an optimist. More importantly, I've discovered why being an optimist hasn't just described my outlook on life – it's actually shaped the life I lead for the better.

I see opportunity where others see struggle. I imagine a comeback when others prematurely mourn a defeat. I settle on a great idea and run with it. I value the strengths in others and refuse to dwell on their weaknesses. I include instead of exclude.

People will tell me all the time that I should play the lottery. I'm *lucky*. It's become a trait like optimism. Everything I touch turns to gold because God wills it, as the myth goes. I used to think I was lucky too. For some reason, the link between my *optimism* and my *luck* was never clear to me before.

It turns out, you can manipulate the direction of your life simply by letting things happen. If you believe the world is flat, you never fall off because you stay off the edge. That's a negative example, but I hope you get the point. Your attitude affects the way your story unfolds. Your life is a self-fulfilling prophesy.

By a positive belief, I don't mean a fanciful wish. I don't mean you can dream of success, and success will just fall into your lap. Don't be fooled or lulled into the false critique of optimism. Optimism takes hard work. It's not about ignoring failures or difficulties. It's about valuing them for what they are. Luck can be a heart attack if you change your bad habits because of it which leads to a healthier life.

I'm not immune from negative experiences. My paternal grandmother became mentally ill and had to be institutionalized with schizophrenia and bipolar disorder. I'm not sure what positivity could have done for her, but I know that being angry or resentful wasn't helpful. I didn't get into medical school on my first try. I was depressed for a time. But I took the opportunity I had to apply again after my last year of college, and now I'm a very successful physician.

Those who believe in the impossible are ridiculed and belittled. These days, our culture loves to laugh at the sarcastic dig much more than it enjoys imagining positive change. Don't allow your life to be dictated by the naysayers.

I've been a happy guy. I've been successful in my life – not just financially but spiritually, emotionally, professionally, and interpersonally. Looking forward, I expect that to continue and I act as it will. That's what worked for me, and I know it can work for many of you.

Just believe in the positive and you can will yourself to be happy in the face of some pretty difficult things. That's not to say you'll never be sad or depressed. Optimism isn't a cure all, but it's the best approach out there. Why not aim for the top?

Live with No Regrets

A friend of mine recently turned me on to a book by Bonnie Ware called *The Top Five Regrets of the Dying*. Ware is an Australian hospice nurse who spent years caring for patients in their final 12 weeks of life. Her reflections are truly a gift for anyone willing to listen. I've summarized them here below.

Regret # 1. I wish I'd had the courage to live a life true to myself, not the life others expected of me...

Ware cites as the most common regret of all, "When people realize that their life is almost over and look back clearly on it, it is easy to see how many dreams have gone unfulfilled."

Regret # 2. I wish I hadn't worked so hard...

Many of Ware's patients missed important moments with their children and their partner. As a father of four myself, I can relate. Kids grow up quickly. When you are trying to earn money with an eye toward the next big purchase – a house, college, sports car – you lose sight of the here and now. It can be easy to lose valuable time. You have to be smart about how you distribute the precious minutes of your day. An extra accolade or nicer car isn't usually worth the sacrifice. Balance!

Regret # 3. I wish I had the courage to express my feelings...

Ware explains that anxiety, stress, and frustration of holding things in were contributing factors to physical illness to some. You were put on this earth for a reason. If you don't express yourself, you might be missing your opportunity to fulfill your purpose. Be true to yourself and speak your truth. Being honest saves time and reduces the risk of misunderstanding. I think Ware's patients realized they'd wasted hours, months, and even years by sometimes failing to express themselves. Don't let that be you!

Regret # 4. I wish I had stayed in touch with my friends...

According to Ware, "Everyone misses their friends when they are dying." Friendships are the roots which sustain you. You start to wilt away if you don't keep them alive. Ask yourself, "Have I been spending sufficient time with my family and friends?" Countless studies have now proven that the number one factor contributing to human happiness is the strength of close friendships. For example, the *American Journal of Public Health* published a study of over 24,000 workers and determined that men and women with the weakest social ties were the most likely to suffer from major depressive symptoms. You need to make friends as part of your life. It's for your own health!

Regret # 5. I wish I had let myself be happier...

Ware describes this as a surprisingly *common* regret. Many of her patients discovered late in life that happiness is actually a choice, and they kicked themselves for failing so often to make that choice. They recognized that they had been trapped by old habits and routines. The comfort of familiarity weighed them down and kept them from exploring the world's full potential.

We tend to believe that happiness occurs in step with pleasurable occurrences. I believe it's more subtle than that. You can find your true happiness once you sense your purpose and meaning in life. Don't forget to look for these. It might help you avoid wishing you had let yourself be happier in the end. Be happy with your life's journey.

Conclusion

In the end, Ware's book challenges us to live according to what we want in life. Now is the time to change for the better – not on your deathbed. We are only given one chance to live out our destiny to both enjoy the world for all its marvelous opportunities and to leave a mark on it in a positive way.

Be the Source of Your Experience

I believe the Universe operates in a deliberate manner and that it provides us with laws. These laws are unfailing. They prohibit mistakes and accidents, and everything in the universe obeys the rules, down to the last atom. So, what does that mean for us?

The principle law of the universe is the *Law of Cause and Effect* which states that for every effect there is a definite cause. Likewise, for every cause, there is a definite effect. Your thoughts, behaviors, and actions create specific effects that manifest and create the life as you know it.

By taking responsibility for what you create in each moment, you begin to realize that your very own experience in life is determined by precisely what you think and feel. And, whether you take conscious control or not of your creation, your experience is based on this law.

You are consumed by whatever motivates you, whether it be desire, jealously, fear, pride, joy, happiness, generosity, etc. The world around you is transfigured into this likeness, as the law operates on what you are putting out into the world.

If you believe your life to be a terrible mess, your life will be a terrible mess. It will become hard to see a way out. However, life will reveal its astonishing nature if you feel strongly that it is breathtaking, abundant, and beautiful. It will be difficult to see it any other way.

As for me, I don't own a pair of rose-tinted shades so I see the world just as well as anyone else does. I see evil in the world, but I also see the beauty and the goodness. However, our experience is a consequence of our collective thinking. Just imagine what our world would be like if each one of us generated lovely thoughts. The whole world would be positively altered.

Be the very source of your experience. You have a force inside of you that creates. Generate good thoughts. Put out good works. Love others. Then see what returns to you. I guarantee you that your life won't be void if you do this. As the late American minister, Norman Vincent Peale, once said:

> *"Change your thoughts and you change the world."*

Share Your Testimony

Working tirelessly to achieve life's goals with purpose doesn't come without milestones. Those milestones also range in importance. They are rewards for the effort you have given. However, those milestones are not the only rewards. Growth and maturation partner with the accomplishment of those goals and, if you're lucky, you'll undergo a complete transformation.

Before working on your goals, you look at your life and take inventory – wondering what you already have to help you towards your transformation process. You ask yourself:

> *"Do I have passion, compassion, and a desire to help others? Am I healthy? Do I need to lose weight? What parts of me do I need to work on? Spiritual? Mental? Physical?"*

You reach for and utilize those inner qualities as you begin working on your goals. You make time for people in ways you never did before. You continue to learn by reading books, and you nurture internal feelings of independence. You put aside thoughts of ever becoming a bodybuilder and focus on what's truly important physically, which is being healthy on a daily basis. You gain an attitude of youthfulness regardless of your chronological age.

New courage comes after reaching each milestone, and this courage strengthens your passion, drive, and will to live. Reaching your goals make you realize that you have strength where you thought weakness only existed.

Your life is more complete – fulfilled. You're rewarded with new friends, self-confidence, a healthier body, and a love for life. You found filled the gaps of your life's puzzle that were missing, and you can move forward basking in the reward of your accomplishments. You may even want to share your testimony to the world. Having others learn from you, after all, would be a great honor.

Embrace Your Story

Most novels won't make sense if you rip out a chapter or two, and this is something many of us try to do with our own lives. The feeling of guilt or pain makes us want to erase the past. I too have tried to disown parts of my life that were painful, difficult, and sad.

As I grow, however, I have come to realize that trying to whitewash pieces of the past doesn't make any more sense than tearing random pages out of a book. Our personalities are forged by our mistakes, as well as our successes.

Struggling through the dark days is the only thing that allows us to recognize the light. Don't try to edit your past. Embrace your story. Every last chapter of it!

Part 5 –
Social Obligations &
Truths

Be Mindful of Who You Follow

The ancient Greek philosopher, Aristotle, was perhaps the first to extol the wisdom of the *crowd*. He was a smart man, and there is certainly something to the idea that collective thinking can yield better and more reasonable thinking in many situations.

However, Aristotle described *mob* mentality to be the flip side of the coin. Just as aggregating opinions and beliefs can lead to a more nuanced analysis, complacency and anonymity within large groups can yield massive errors and even atrocities.

History is filled with stories of the weak-willed who followed the crowd over the proverbial cliff. Nazi Germany might be one striking case, but our daily lives are full of far more banal examples. It's easy not to think if we are simply doing what everyone else is doing.

Be mindful of who you follow and be intentional about why you're following them. Don't be afraid to question the so-called wisdom of the crowds. When you know you're right, don't be afraid to strike out responsibly. Otherwise, you might find yourself walking blindly off a cliff.

Become a Great Leader

Recent events have brought many tragic circumstances to my country, the United States of America. They have been less than cheerful for so many, and they have made me think about what makes a *true* leader.

The late Peter Drucker, an Austrian-born American management consultant, once said:

> *"The only definition of a leader is someone who has followers."*

That definition, in my opinion, is too simplistic and possibly dangerous. So, what makes a great leader?

The dictionary defines a leaders as:

> *"The one in charge, the person who convinces other people to follow. A great leader inspires confidence in other people and moves them to action."*

I agree with that definition. In my opinion, great leaders exhibit the following qualities:

- A great leader is able to set out a compelling vision that engages his or her team.

- A great leader communicates his or her vision clearly, simply, powerfully, and often.

- A great leader is driven by principles and greater purpose – not self-aggrandizement or ego.

- A great leader takes a stance of serving the people he or she leads rather than depending on his or her position of authority.

- A great leader makes decisions because he or she believes they are the right decisions, not just the popular decisions.

- A great leader ensures that his or her leadership team is aligned around the same goal.

- A great leader is emotionally intelligent and looks for the long-term win-win.

- A great leader leads by example and actions.

- A great leader only gives a speech to change the world (something the 35th President of the United States, John F. Kennedy, once said).

Don't Neglect Value

It's not often that I get to join my family for a nice brunch, but I took the time to accompany them on one fantastic morning. As I was in the buffet line, I got to thinking about the cost. If an all-you-can-eat pass allows me to eat whatever I want, I should get my money's worth. Right? My logic made the buffet worth the deal.

The buffet really seemed like a great deal in comparison to the fancy and expensive meals I've experienced with many of the very influential medical and fitness leaders in my business industry. Dining at the most amazing five star restaurants, I've been blessed with their generosity. My last two meals were well over $100 each and, yet, I managed to walk out without feeling stuffed.

These haute cuisine dinners included some of the most delicious foods I've ever tasted. Quite frankly, the entire experience was out of this world each time. Even so, I found myself upset about it. There was just no way that my dinners could have cost so much money as I wasn't even stuffed to the gills. I just couldn't understand the logic.

Every business in America is competing with other businesses, fighting to get the most they can out of every penny they spend – profit above all else. As individuals, we're similar as most of us like to rationalize the way we spend our money, especially in terms of perceived value.

However, many of these businesses neglect the value they can add to society through quality care, service, and experience. As consumers, we are no less culpable. We are often asking ourselves how we can get the most bang for our buck. I've heard it all.

> *"Where can I get jammed stuffed for only twenty bucks? I want to try it all without paying a premium!"*

When it comes to buffet dining, I am the number one offender. I go crazy while cramming food onto my plate. I even go back to the bar two or three times because I want to be sure I'm getting my money's worth. It's addictive.

This made me take a step back and ponder.

In America, an obesity epidemic is running rampant. There's no two ways about it. It's serious, and it's in our face every day. This crisis may be even more pronounced being I'm in the medical profession. Nevertheless, our decreasing health standards are causing a deterioration in our children's lives, and our loved ones will die younger.

As consumers and business people, we have to stand up for life and stop thinking about *getting more to pay less*. Instead, consider the outcomes.

> *"Do I really need this food? Is it safe to put this food in my body? Are the extra pounds of food per dollar worth my health in the long run?"*

I'm not saying that dining out at a buffet is wrong. It may be okay every once in a great while, though it isn't the wisest choice if you're in desperate need of losing weight and getting healthy.

Think of *quality over quantity*. Some of my most amazing experiences I've had at high-quality restaurants were not characterized by mountainous plates of food or huge variety. The restaurants served quality in the way of food, but they also provided superior service and unique ambiance.

So, what is the true value of a product? What benefits you the most? Stop thinking in *bulk* terms. A deal can sometimes be the wrong deal if it's not quality.

Share the Wealth

It seems that wealth is a dirty word these days. As many Americans struggle to make ends meet, we vilify the richest of the rich who seem to represent what is selfish and hedonistic. However, wealth can be something more than a dirty word. In fact, wealth consciousness can lead to abundance for all.

Wealth consciousness is about so much more than simply having the ability to make more and accumulate more wealth. It's not about luxury and excess. It's about a strongly held belief that what we truly need, our own abundance is always available to us if we are mindful of it.

Wealth is more than a dirty word to bifurcate the haves from the have-nots. Wealth extends to every aspect of life – health, relationships, spirituality, and connection to the Universe and our Creator.

I firmly believe that we are all meant to live with abundance. It's not a zero-sum game. Wealth consciousness is a mentality that attracts all of life' potential abundance and helps us to enjoy the fullness of our own potential.

We must focus on what matters and grab what is there for the taking while sharing what's there to be shared. As we stop thinking of wealth in terms of dollars and cents, we can begin to think of wealth in terms of spiritual and emotional abundance. As Confucius once said:

> *"In a country well governed, poverty is something to be ashamed of. In a country badly governed, wealth is something to be ashamed of."*

Abundance is a state of mind. May we adopt a mentality of wealth as a lifestyle as we all deserve it.

Don't Fight the World

It seems like we spend a lot of time creating divisions among people where there really do not need to be divisions. Instead of looking for ways to cooperate with others so that we all can win, we look for ways to compete so that there is only one *winner* and everyone else is a *loser*.

From politics to business, it seems that our culture has evolved into constant struggle against *the other*. Instead of collaborating, we erect walls and stake out artificial divisions. Instead of aiming for the best possible solution, we fight to win which often, if not always, means we try to ensure that someone loses.

A friend of mine pointed out this same absurdity in the *Hunger Games* series. The fictional teen character, Katniss Everdeen, and her family are in a very *us versus them* situation with regards to the tyrannical dictatorship setting of the *Capitol* city. It resides in Panem, a country with a totalitarian government and 12 districts. The Capitol treats those in the districts as objects for entertainment by forcing a youth from each one of the districts to compete in a nationally televised event called the *Hunger Games*. Instead of everyone working together to create a great society, each youth must fight to the death in order to survive. Katniss is one of the youth that must survive.

Believe it or not, the world of health and fitness engages in unnecessary conflict as well. Many of the clients I work with feel locked in a struggle against food, as well as the forces preventing them from exercising. But, there's another way to look at things. We must ask ourselves:

> *"How can we coexist with things that don't always agree with our sensibilities?"*

Instead of bemoaning the fact that a restaurant offers poutine and hamburger, maybe we should ask the waiter what they can cook up with broccoli and grilled chicken. You'd be surprised how eager restaurants are to collaborate.

Instead of hating your job for taking so much time out of your day that you find it difficult to exercise, perhaps you use your office as a mini-gym. Each day, find how often you can take extra steps, do squats, pushups, or run up and down the stairs.

Don't fight the world. Work within it. Work with others. Don't seek out conflict when you can enjoy the harmony of collaboration.

Improve the World

The world-famous German-born diarist and World War II Holocaust victim, Anne Frank once said:

> *"How wonderful it is that nobody need wait a single moment before starting to improve the world."*

That quote was incredibly insightful for a child of 15 years. She was absolutely right. We don't need to wait a single moment to improve the world, nor do we have to wait a single moment to improve our chances for success.

If we wait for the *perfect moment*, we can bet it will be too late. After all, life gets in the way. We create more excuses, and our goals keep getting shoved to the back burner.

So, forget about waiting for the perfect moment to begin because that moment is NOW. Stop making excuses. Stop wanting for Mondays. Stop waiting to volunteer.

We all make mistakes, but we all have the ability to overcome. Be insightful like little Anne Frank.

Treasure Values

Your values are not your beliefs. In a nutshell, values belong to your soul while beliefs belong to your mind.

Values are your spiritual DNA. Your values, and the way you exercise them, are the expression of your souls. They inform your life's calling, and they fuel your potential.

Beliefs are a little different. They are ideas which are often adopted unopposed from your environment. You establish your beliefs that have been passed down from various sources of authority.

Think about your own life. Have you accepted your beliefs as an absolute truth just because they've never truly been challenged? Do you sometimes believe what you believe just because you have always believed it? Is it because your parents believe it or because it's a commonly held belief in your culture, neighborhood, or society?

If you make the mistake of equating these inherited beliefs with your core values, you risk losing your creative power and inner truths. Values are the foundation upon which you build a fulfilling and meaningful life.

You did not create most of the things you believe about yourself and your reality. Every incident in your life is by nature, neutral in its potential to affect you positively or negatively. You endow these events with meanings based on your beliefs. If you want change in your life, you have to start by changing the beliefs that don't serve you.

This is the responsibility that true value entail. You have to take ownership over the creation of every moment's feeling. Your experience is going to be generated whether you take control of these beliefs or not. Once you acknowledge the ways in which your automatic and subconscious belief systems shape your experience, you'll be so much better able to redirect your beliefs to align with our inner values. You'll be happier because you will have shaped your experience out of your own internal happiness.

Check Your Belief System

Sometimes, deeply held beliefs breed negative things like racial prejudice and discrimination. This system of hatred can be appealing to some because they exploit deep emotional insecurities, jealousy, and fear.

We must free ourselves from negative and limited belief systems in order to appreciate the truth and to see reality clearly and untainted by discord. In order to evolve, we must change the way we see the world and our place in it.

Many of today's most outspoken characters rally behind destructive belief systems. They feed off prejudices and preconceptions. They hide facts behind stereotypes. They ridicule love with cynical barbs. They mock optimism and idealism by trumpeting trepidation. They hate hope because they have none.

If a person believes a thing like the inferiority of another race, he will see signs that validate his perspective. Our brains are tricky. They can fool us into thinking our fears and prejudices are confirmed by what we think we see all around us. If we aren't careful, our brains allow us to see the world through lenses colored by our own limiting beliefs.

Don't be fooled. Every once in a while, shed your lenses and take a clean look around. If your beliefs lead you to hate, it's time for new beliefs.

Be a Part of Community

I once had a patient that told me she was *spiritual but not religious*. Like me, she grew up in the Catholic faith. As she grew older, she became disenchanted and felt weighed down by the tradition of Christianity. She went further, claiming that she had been emotionally damaged by it. The rituals, preaching, and interactions with fellow parishioners became rather boring and disappointing. I gathered that she was disappointed because she was yearning for something deeper, perhaps a sense of fulfillment that was not found in church rituals.

After several attempts to find her inner peace in different religious organizations, this woman finally gave up and opted for staying home on Sunday mornings. She preferred to read the Sunday newspaper while enjoying a cup of her favorite java. Other Sundays, she put on her running shoes and go for a run.

While running, my patient experienced a unique connection with nature which she equated to a profound religious experience, as well as her own personal encounter with God. She said that it was there that she realized that she was spiritual but not religious.

As I listened to her, I recalled my own spiritual journey as I had also been consumed by a similar philosophy. My religion became worshipping exercise as I talked with God on my morning runs through the park. I became a well-meaning and a spiritual Sunday jogger as I constructed a religion of my own making. Perhaps this is what my patient had done as well.

The God of spirituality is found by us, as well as on our own terms. It is like knowing a person from outside before we let the person speak. Thus, we understand the person according to our own interpretation. Suddenly then, that person speaks and immediately overwhelms the perception we had in mind. God is not a distant Being. Yes, we are spiritual seekers, but God seeks us above all.

I often hear folks lament the rules and rigidity of organized religion. It's often the reason these folks have stopped going to church. I think the complaint reflects a preference for more comfortable, private relationships with God. In those complaints, I cannot help but hear, "I don't want to be bothered with the salvation of others as that is their own personal issue." It's the consumer approach to religion.

Religion is not only about rules and regulations. It's also about service, growth, social work, prayers, and ultimately salvation.

The entire world is institutionalized, and institutions are essential for society to survive. Yes, there some institutions that are corrupt, unfair, and inefficient. However, we must remember that those institutions are made of people just like you and me. Without institutions, it would be impossible to accomplish anything. There would be no public schools or universities, government-run hospitals or health clinics, private medical facilities, or investment banks. The pure essence of our society would evaporate.

In fairness, this issue is a two-way street. There are other individuals who claim to be religious but are not interested in the spiritual component of their religion. They become obsessed with following norms, rules, and laws without questions or compassion. They believe that if they follow all these rules, they will secure their place in salvation and earn some sort of *very important person (VIP)* pass into Heaven. These people are also not interested in what happens to others. They are judgmental, and they don't believe in kindness and service to others unless it benefits them directly.

Institutions are imperfect, and organized religions are institutions. At times, they serve the interests of corruption and evil. More often, they produce the benefits of communion, shared faith, and care. Reform comes from individuals engaging in the institutions and is harmed when we choose to turn our backs and ignore our communities of faith.

Participation is a key to spirituality. In helping others, we discern our purpose and accomplish our mission on earth. We learn to live for others and not just for ourselves. Worshipping God in public keeps us honest and confirms our values.

Remember, God doesn't need worship. However, we do need to worship Him.

Correct Political Correctness

The current political atmosphere in the United States is comfortable endorsing politicians that have bucked the vagaries of conventional politicking and promote a culture of aggressive political incorrectness. They are willing to say what many don't want to hear:

> *"Tell it like it is."*

Recently, I had to perform a series of four or five medical procedures back to back. I wasn't nervous about the procedures themselves, especially since I've performed similar ones thousands of times. However, I did face a unique challenge this time.

All my patients were seriously overweight. This made a normally simple procedure become a complex maneuver. Even with the state-of-the-art imaging machines, I couldn't see the needle I was using for the procedure due to all the excess fat and skin on my patients.

Besides the technical challenge, these patients caused me to find myself over and over again in a very human conundrum. If I was one of those politicians, I might say:

> "You're fat! You're so fat, that you're going to die young. If you don't take control of your life, there is very little I can do for you. I can't be blamed if this procedure doesn't go well because you're so fat. It would have been an easy procedure, but it's not because of your fat. That's tough luck for you."

Most of my patients wouldn't be amused with that tone or verbiage, even the ones who support that kind of politician.

Of course, it never occurred to me to say anything like that. I don't think it would occur to most of us. I have counseled a few people to lose a little weight, but I didn't add the urgency so explicitly.

So, why are so many people attracted to that type of behavior in politicians? Why would I be criticized or fired for doing what they do? Are we happy to hear them attacking or insulting others? Do we not want to be the subject ourselves to the same kind of bluntness?

But, is there a role for bluntness in our lives? Is there a place where being too polite or too politically correct isn't doing anyone any good? Including my patients? How do we choose what to tiptoe around and what to challenge head on?

Master the Brain

It was another beautiful day in Safety Harbor, Florida. I had recently returned from vacation. The sky-blue bay gleamed with sunlight as I walked carelessly under the generous shade of impressive willow trees. I wanted to run and to feel the air whiz by my ears. The birds could have been chirping my favorite exercise mix for all I knew. I was euphoric.

And then I heard it – a gravelly voice stopping and starting in fits, like shotgun blasts. As I climbed a slight hill, the voice became louder. In the distance, I spotted a man walking his dog. He was dressed in a jacket too warm for the weather. His left fist was clenched as he tugged and pulled at his small dog's short leash. The dog yelped in opposition.

I could not understand what the man was shouting. All I heard was anger. His head swiveled back and forth along the manicured bushes lining the path. He pointed sinisterly at them. As I got closer, I realized he wasn't pointing – his thumb was cocked and loaded. His index finger fired away. He was shooting at the bushes with his hand while making firing noises and crackling. He screamed profanities maniacally at his imaginary targets. I turned and ran the other way.

It was clear the man I saw was deranged. He likely had some sort of mental illness and was disturbed. More on that in a second.

My first thought was, "How could this man be so angry?" Surrounded by the sounds of a blossoming spring, warmed by some of the kindest sunshine I have ever felt, and embraced by lushness – why was he so mad?

His day wasn't beautiful. He didn't feel euphoric. We were in the same place and looking at the same thing, yet we were worlds apart. We experienced a vastly different reality.

I spend a lot of time thinking about my physical fitness. A lot of us do. We are rightly concerned about the negative impacts of our unhealthy lifestyles. Unfortunately, we often neglect our mental health.

Our experiences may not be as extreme as the troubled man in the park, but some kind of mental illness is a possibility that all can suffer from time to time. Our reality is shaped by our perception, and our perceptions are colored by our attitudes and our overall mental health.

Our brains are the masters of our reality. If we're lucky enough to have some control over it, we need to take care of our minds and be intentional about how we experience and react to the world. We can't see the sunshine if our brains are shrouded in darkness. We must keep an open mind and a positive attitude while letting the light flood in. We must program our brains.

Comfort the Depressed

Immediately after the unexpected death of Robin Williams, the comedian actor, hundreds of posts on social media inundated us about his decision to prematurely end his life. I am sure many of you observed, as I did at the time, that some of these posts judged his suicide as an act of cowardice or selfishness. Celebrating his life, the argument seemed to go, validated his choice to end it.

Many people asked:

> "How can someone, who appeared to be so fortunate and so successful, commit such a desperate act? With all the treasures Robin Williams enjoyed throughout his life, who was he to be depressed? What gave him the right to throw away such privilege when so many of us are struggling?"

I have to say that the debate struck a chord with me. Those judgments were misguided and simply wrong, in my opinion.

It's not necessarily their fault, but those people just don't understand depression. Being depressed isn't about being sad. It's about losing your purpose. It's about losing your hope and your lust for life. It's a chemical imbalance, and it's a failure of the human psyche. It is, in the truest sense of the word, an illness.

Suicide is generally the product of severe depression. The Centers for Disease Control suggests that nearly one in 10 Americans are suffering the effects of some sort of depression right this minute. Depression is truly an epidemic.

On this, I speak from experience. I, like many Americans, have felt lonely and defeated even while being surrounded by a loving family and experiencing professional success. Though I certainly can't say that I sunk to the depths of Robin Williams' despair, the thought of death being a welcome consolation for my depression has crossed my mind more than once.

The illness of depression cuts away at humanity. It makes one question the motivation for hanging on to life – and don't be fooled – life requires us to hang on. Sometimes, the hanging on is too difficult for those people who suffer from severe depression. In fact, the pain and symptoms of depression often makes it difficult to ask for help.

For many who suffer depression, religion can pull them out of the disease. For others, it's the support of family. For some, it is medical treatment and therapy. For all those who survive the disease, it takes the kindness and understanding of others. Negativity doesn't help anyone. Judgment is cheap.

We should all take Robin William's death as a call for action instead.

One out of every 10 people who interacts with us on a daily basis is likely depressed. We need to take the time to understand their pain, show them that life is worth living, and that there is a purpose in life. We need to take the time to see their sadness even as they try to hide it with jokes and smiles and work. Robin Williams is a great example of how the most animated people, even those with seemingly so much going for him, can be living in silence with these demons.

Suicide is not an option. It's an act of severe desperation. Instead of judging those who succumb to depression, let's take the steps to help them avoid becoming victims of that depressive state in which they find themselves. Let's look for the positive in the world and share it with others so that they, too, can discover a renewed sense of purpose. Let's make sure that those in our lives who struggle silently can feel safe in asking us for help. That's the lesson to draw from the tragedy of the ending of Robin William's life.

Have Compassion

This week, a co-worker and dear friend of mine lost his daughter to suicide, the end case after a tough battle with depression. It was especially hard to fathom since I had seen how committed my friend was day in and day out to support his daughter through tough times. As a father of four myself, I cannot begin to imagine the pain he feels each moment he lives without this piece of himself.

During this difficult time, it seemed every news alert on my phone has been about another celebrity who had taken his or her own life – another soul passed on to heaven. However, news alerts are distant stories captured in cyberspace behind glass screens. A few days ago, that glass divider was shattered for me as my friend suffered his great loss.

As depression cuts short the life of so many beautiful people, I cannot help but to hope that the renewed focus resulting from these tragedies will help sensitize our society to mental health. Could these individuals who suffer feel uplifted by compassionate communities that defeat negative perceptions and stigmas associated with mental illness?

For these individuals, the path to suicide was not necessarily short. Though these men, women, and children live in our very public world, they struggle often in private. We, as a society, have a responsibility to help them.

So many of us are fixated on appearance as we want to look strong while forgetting that strength and bravery are, often times, born by acknowledging our vulnerabilities. When we fail to recognize our own struggles and let others know that we too feel the way they do, we fail them. We make them feel alone and like a unique burden on the world. This leads to hopelessness.

Depression can be difficult to spot. Unlike a cut or a bruise, there is no blood stain or mark. However, the pain is real. We wouldn't let a friend bleed out right next to us without offering a bandage. We wouldn't make a relative on crutches carry her on bags. So, don't be blind to depression.

I speak from experience. I like so many Americans, have suffered the pangs of depression through loneliness and isolation. Plus, I felt guilty on top of feeling sad. I had the privilege of having a loving family and caring friends. Yet, I hardened my exterior and didn't deal with my emotions. I could have become a statistic myself if I wouldn't have addressed my pain. Thankfully, I never sunk to the deepest depths of depression. However, the thought of suicide did cross my mind. It can seem like a welcome relief when a world seems so hostile. I share this to let you know that you are not alone.

If you're ever incline to judge someone who's committed suicide, I hope that you will wait before passing judgment. Just look deep inside yourself and try to understand what horrible pain that person must have felt. Naturally, our bodies are programmed to preserve life. Suicide goes against nature, so you should know that something very serious went wrong for this person to go to this depth.

A tragedy is an event unto itself. You can process it, grieve, and appreciate a life gone. Looking for reasons is meaningless, as you may never understand the mind of someone in such despair. However, telling your own story and listening to the stories of others may help. Create yourself in the image of compassion. Everyone can use a little more love.

Thank Our Veterans

As a psychiatrist, my father spent his entire career working as a civilian for the United States Navy and Veterans Administration (VA) hospitals, treating service members and veterans for over 20 years. After I became a doctor myself, I chose to do my residency in a VA hospital as well. Both my father and I were touched tremendously by the service and sacrifice of our patients, and we tried in our small measure to give back.

On Veterans Day 1987, I brought home my first son. Who knew that, years later, he would be a commissioned officer in the United States Navy too! After having been around our service members and veterans for so long, I know how important my son's decision was to volunteer. Like him, I am grateful for all those who have raised their hands and pledged to protect and defend our country.

It's a robust lineage of honor to have members of my family help our veterans. Most of all, I honor those who serve in our military. I hope that you will join me in thanking them. When you're strolling through the town, be sure to thank you fellow soldiers.

Honor the Soldiers

Memorial Day is a day to remember the very real sacrifices that were made by those in military who served our country, the United States of America. They were the ones who gave their lives as the ultimate sacrifice to save us from terror, violence, and indecency in the world.

Several years ago, I visited the Tomb of the Unknown Soldier in Washington, DC. The Soldiers and Marines who guard it marched silently, precisely in unison and with great pride with each step and every choreographed maneuver. They march in the snow, under the rain, and through the blistering heat. It brought to mind Aristotle's maxim.

> *"We are what we repeatedly do. Excellence then is not an act but a habit."*

Those service members who put themselves in harm's way for us didn't live fleeting moments of intensity and courage. They forged their honor and excellence through years of discipline, precision, consistency, and selflessness. Those habits and rituals were the truest expression of their character.

Memorial Day is not just a day for us to only remember the ultimate sacrifices of our service men and women. Let us remember all the *little* daily sacrifices they made, as well as the painstaking precision with which they lived their careers and lives – like the soldiers who marched at the Tomb of the Unknown. Let's draw inspiration from their example and value commitment and consistency over short-term intensity.

Even more, let us pray for today's soldiers who put themselves in harm's way for our glory. Let us show true appreciation for their service and sacrifice. May we say *thank you* to all those who are paying the highest price for our freedom, as well as to their families that raised such courageous and selfless human beings.

Celebrate Good Workers

Labor Day is a day to honor the American labor movement. During this holiday, we pay tribute to the workers who have contributed enormously to the strength, prosperity, and wellbeing of our country.

What Happens if Jobs Go Away?

I want you to consider this. It is estimated that 70 to 80 percent of the current jobs are going to disappear in the next 20 years. Don't get me wrong. There will be a lot of other *new* jobs, but is not clear if there will be *enough* jobs in such a limited time for everybody – especially if robots are doing the work.

What does this mean socially? Automation doesn't necessarily mean the equal distribution of wealth. I'm not saying it should, so don't get me wrong. That's a whole new conversation for another day. The question is, "What happens to all the people who can't find a job or aren't needed to work?" Obviously, less money and more struggle will occur for many.

Hopefully, more countries will be as forward thinking as China. To keep their citizens employed, they have provided jobs in building a canal across the country. This is being done by hand rather than machines which may seem inefficient, but it is understandable knowing they could have a job problem in the future.

Has Good Labor Gone by the Wayside?

Recently, I decided to install hardwood floors in my master bedroom. This is something I've contemplated since building the house 17 years ago, so I hired a handyman to do the job. I've known this man for more than 15 years.

Before hiring, I asked the man if he was capable of doing the entire job in a professional manner. After all, it was the first time that he was faced with a higher-end job like this. The type of wood floor I wanted installed required it to be glued to the floor.

During most of the process, the installation went well with no major setbacks. That is, until we got to the final stage of the job. I decided to remove one of the newly installed moldings around some marble tiles because it didn't look right.

To my surprise, the wood ends were unevenly cut. This didn't matter to the handyman because he felt the molding wouldn't be seen. He asked, "Why waste my time finishing the trim properly if no one was going to see it?" Needless to say, I got upset with him.

This reminded me of when I first built my house 17 years ago when a contractor was installing a tile floor in the kitchen. When he got to the space where the dishwasher was to be installed, he insinuated that it was not necessary to lay down tiles in this space because no one was going to ever see it. So, why should I waste time and money if this contractor wasn't going to do the job properly? After all, this was a job I was paying him for.

Isn't a Job Worth Doing Right?

I once read an anecdote from Steve Jobs' biography by Walter Isaacson. As the American entrepreneur and cofounder of Apple, Inc., Steve talked about an obsession he had in making sure that all Apple iPhones and computers were made properly with the interior being painted and finished. Though he knew nobody was going to see the interior of the phone, he still wanted them complete.

From his father, Steve learned about good work. When he was a child, he and his father built a fence together. They were finishing the back of the fence, an area that nobody was going to ever see. Steve was curious and asked his father why they should do this. His father told him that he loved doing things right and that he even cared about the look of parts nobody couldn't see. Steve admired his father for this.

> "Although my Dad didn't raise a billionaire, he is a craftsmen and a painter and he instilled in me the same love of details, even those some may think inconsequential. He taught me to wash the undersides of car's rocker panels and the engine compartment,

things I still do today. I fully believe that
the impression my father made on me
about the importance of the details has
been one of the major components of
whatever success I've had as a writer and
photographer."

Jobs would recall the lessons taught by his father about the attention worth paying, even to the things unseen, throughout his career and life.

Honor Those Who Take Pride in Good Work

Recently, I've been studying the Old Testament. In Joshua 6:20-21, it reads:

"Therefore, with all the people shouting,
and trumpets blaring, after the voice and
the sound increased in the ears of the
multitude, the walls promptly fell to ruin.
And they seized the city."

Did God take advantage of the poorly built walls to let the people of Israel conquer the city? Did people in Jericho pay the ultimate price because their builders had the same mentality as my handyman in cutting corners because nobody was going to see their work?

Although the consequences might not be cataclysmic, I hope that you celebrate Labor Day by appreciating the past, as well as the present, workers who took or take pride in their work. Fight and advocate for those who have provided quality work for you – those who have built for you, your business, or your country.

Workers who took pride in building the foundation of this country are those we honor today. Their work might not be obvious, but it is appreciated and necessary. I am hopeful and thankful for the future of our country that will continually be built upon by dedicated and thoughtful laborers.

Praise Nurses

Though there is a week that celebrates nurses – *National Nurses Week* – we should praise them every week. After all, nurses make a positive impact in the lives of those in their care. Year round, nurses save lives. In non-life threatening cases, their dedicated attention touches the hearts of their patients and family members.

As a doctor, I see this every day. As a father, I especially experienced the kindness and care of nurses when I walked with my youngest son into our surgery center in the hopes of curing his back pain.

The first person who greeted my son was a nurse. It was 5 o'clock in the morning, and the nurses overlooked my poor bedside manners. Just as I had seen the nurses do so many times in my profession, they walked my son through each step of the care process. Something struck me then. It was at that moment that I finally understood the compassion of nurses.

The nurses were able to help my son relax and get comfortable as he ventured into his new environment. Without them, I can't even imagine how afraid my son could have been. The good thing is I don't have to. I am just thankful each day for their compassion.

Be sure to thank your nurses for the excellent service of healing and caring they bring to your lives. They truly embody the healing edge of caring.

Overcome Tragedy with Hope

In the aftermath of recent world tragedies, I am sure that millions around the world are asking themselves how God can allow so many innocent people to suffer so often. It's a question I struggled with after flying to Haiti a few years ago following that island's devastating earthquake.

As soon as I stepped out of the plane and onto the makeshift tarmac, the stench of rotting corpses nearly bowled me over. The limbless and the starving were strewn along the streets awaiting their turn to be seen by a doctor or an aid worker.

On my first day in the mobile clinic, I met an 8-year old boy who had been lucky to survive only to discover that his 10 family members had been fatally buried in the rubble. From time to time, I could hear rustling beneath piles of dust and cement as I walked by plots of land where buildings had once stood, and I would wonder if someone else was still trapped. Many were, but only a few were ultimately rescued.

I am a doctor, so I am not a stranger to death. Still, something about the nature of the tragedy in Haiti seemed cruel and inhumane. What kind of a God could stand by idly as His children were literally being crushed beneath Him? Even more, what sort of God would set this kind of a world in motion to begin with?

At night, I slept with other relief workers in the open air courtyard of a Jesuit monastery. Growing up in the Caribbean, I knew Haiti to be a country teeming with life. However, those nights there were eerily silent and seemingly lifeless.

Late into one of my last nights on the island before the sun began to reveal itself, I was overcome by my doubts. I really couldn't fathom how God could have abandoned an entire country like this.

In the cot beside me, I heard a faint musical whispering. I knew it was coming from one of the American Jesuit missionary brothers. I held my breath while trying to make out the words. Then I realized he was singing *En Mi Viejo San Juan*. It made me want to leap out of my bed as it was a tune I knew well from my youth in Puerto Rico.

It turns out that the missionary brother had spent some time on my home island many years back. The sound of the song inspired me to whisper over to him as he lay awake. He turned over with a smile and I asked him, "How could God allow all this suffering?" If you think about it, this was an importune question. After all, this man had devoted his life to God so he should know the answer, right?

Here in the middle of a disaster area where this man had selflessly volunteered to help and sleep under the stars, I was questioning his faith. He didn't bat an eye though. Almost confused, he asked me, "Why would you ask that kind of question?"

Then he explained and admonished me, "It's not a matter of why God does or doesn't allow things to happen. The real question that should keep you up at night is, 'How do we turn all of this around?'"

I have to say that I was inspired to think about this subject a little more by my Jesuit bunkmate. Our very natural tendency is to think backwards and to wonder, "Why?" The missionary's point is that maybe the only question we can ever really hope to answer is *what*.

> *"What can we do with what we've been given?"*

Goodness between humans rarely comes out of thin air. It is almost always born out of conflict, adversity, or strife.

The efforts in Haiti inspired me to rethink my medical practice. I know that the multiple tragedies that we face almost daily around the world will make things worse before things get better. Instead of asking why would God let it happen, I hope that we choose to ask ourselves, "What does God want us to do about it, and how will our reaction help make this world a better, safer more prosperous one?"

Epilogue

Until Next Time

These anecdotes, stories, and advice are not meant to provide the tools to extinguish any pain or end any difficult journey. After my incredible physical transformation from an unhealthy existence into a lifestyle of fitness and sound nutrition, I simultaneously underwent changes in the way I looked at things.

These short chapters tell the stories of these changes. As patients shared their own stories with me, I was compelled by their human commonality and their uniqueness to share them with you. I realized that if pain is universal, so too could be joy and happiness. If struggles were a common denominator in the lives of many, so too could be triumphs. I wanted to share my journey with you.

I hope that these stories or vignette's provide you with another weapon in the fight against self-doubt or despair. I hope they shine a light on experiences that may seem dark and illuminate shameful corners and expose their hidden beauty.

Writing and sharing my inner thoughts with you has allowed me to tap into those moments in my life when I've been the weakest – those moral dilemmas, the failures and moments of fear that have haunted my experience. Sharing my deepest feelings and emotions with people like you, as well as my moments of triumph, has been therapeutic for me, to say the least.

This is not the end of my story. My body was out of shape. I exercised, improved my nutrition. Then my physical transformation occurred. In the beginning, my mind was doubtful but I persevered. The next part of my journey takes me to my soul. It was also aching. To figure out what it needed, I explored another realm of my identity. I went on to study my religious backgrounds and dug deeply into my spirituality with a newfound mindset. I hope you'll be part of this new journey with me in my next book.

d

Other Books by
Dr. Francisco M. Torres

Dr. T's Drop the Fat Diet

12 Steps to a Leaner You Forever

Several years ago, Dr. T decided to take his life into his own hands. Now you can too with this common-sense, medically-tested, clinically-proven way to jumpstart your metabolism, plan your meals, and get going toward a new you forever. This is not your average weight loss book, and it's not a fad diet. For years, Dr. T has been helping hundreds of his own clients achieve body and wellness transformations as incredible as his own. In this book he shares the secret – a comprehensive and realistic approach to fat loss. The results are proven. The plan is simple. All you have to do is dive in and drop the fat.

12 Practical Steps to a New You Forever

From Shame and Sadness to Sheer Bliss

Life transformation isn't the stuff of fairy tales and misplace hope. Instead, life transformation is real and it's for you, no matter what your own story is or who you may be. Whatever your current status is, or your past, don't let it define you. You are your potential. Don't worry about whether or not you believe you can change. Logic doesn't require your belief. Expect progress instead, as you allow us to assist you in planning a practical approach to weight loss, health, and more.

h

12 Practical Steps to a New You Forever Without Arthritis

Stealing Back Your Life from Pain and Inflammation

While there are many books on arthritis, you can approach this one with appreciation as it provides hope to live and, in fact, thrive despite the disease. This book is a practical set of suggestions, undergirded by a real passion to help all those who contront the effects of arthritis daily. Because seeing your doctor is not always an opion, this book provides a variety of alternative and natural remedies to relieve stiffness and pain.